The Educational Potential of e-Portfolios

Supporting personal development and reflective learning

Lorraine Stefani, Robin Mason and Chris Pegler

Routledge
Taylor & Francis Group

LONDON AND NEW YORK

First published 2007
by Routledge
2 Park Square, Milton Park, Abingdon, Oxon OX14 4RN

Simultaneously published in the USA and Canada
by Routledge
270 Madison Ave, New York, NY 10016

Routledge is an imprint of the Taylor & Francis Group, an informa business

© 2007 Lorraine Stefani, Robin Mason and Chris Pegler

Typeset in Times New Roman by
GreenGate Publishing Services, Tonbridge, Kent
Printed and bound in Great Britain by T J International Ltd, Padstow, Cornwall

British Library Cataloguing in Publication Data
A catalogue record for this book is available from the British Library

Library of Congress Cataloging in Publication Data
Stefani, Lorraine, 1953-
   The educational potential of e-portfolios : supporting personal
   development and reflective learning / Lorraine Stefani, Robin Mason,
   and Chris Pegler.
   p. cm. — (Connecting with e-learning)
   Includes bibliographical references and index.
   ISBN 0-415-41214-5 (pbk.) — ISBN 0-415-41213-7 (hardback) 1.
Electronic portfolios in education. I. Mason, Robin. II. Pegler, Chris, 1956- III.
Title.
   LB1029.P67S74 2007
   379.1'66—dc22
   2006036578

ISBN10: 0-415-41213-7 (hbk)
ISBN10: 0-415-41214-5 (pbk)
ISBN13: 978-0-415-41213-1 (hbk)
ISBN13: 978-0-415-41214-8 (pbk)

Contents

Illustrations

Figures

Tables

Series editors' foreword
The ubiquitous e-portfolio

Portfolios are one of the most adaptable tools currently available to educators around the world. Widespread adoption of portfolios into practice is largely due to their ability to support a range of processes important in Tertiary Education in countries around the world. They are characterised by flexibility and ease of use and ability to be adapted to suit a range of applications. However, the introduction of networked e-portfolios has extended the ways in which information can be accessed, used, updated and integrated, broadening the range of reflective activities that can be supported.

E-portfolios are being used to support a variety of activities related to learning and professional development. They can be used simply to store and organise information. For example, e-portfolios can allow students to arrange materials for assessment, and are used extensively for this purpose in art and design related disciplines. However, e-portfolios are not simply repositories and can be used to support reflection on assessment outcomes. Similarly, e-portfolios can be used as a tool to support reflective learning processes, such as problem based learning, with individual students or teams contributing and integrating information within the portfolio. Recently the use of e-portfolios has extended beyond learning processes into the domain of Professional Development Planning. Here e-portfolio tools can support reflection on professional goals, particularly within the vocational disciplines, such as health professions, education, law and accountancy.

The swift success of e-portfolios has led to limitations, as theory struggles to keep pace with practice. Working within an area of rapid change has been challenging for the authors, but they found a pragmatic solution by focusing on the ways e-portfolios might support a range of processes, using a range of illustrations from practice around the world.

The Educational Potential of e-Portfolios is an essential handbook for educators wishing to explore a variety of uses of e-portfolios. The authors, Lorraine Stefani, Robin Mason and Chris Pegler, were chosen for their theoretical knowledge and practical engagement with learning processes and technologies. Drawing on the experiences of expert practitioners, the book is packed with practical examples from colleagues around the world. The authors cite examples across a range of institutions and countries, offering a readable, non-technical and comprehensive introduction to e-portfolios informed by practice.

The book is one of two texts heralding a new series, 'Connecting with e-learning'. This series is aimed at teachers, academics, librarians, managers and educational support staff who are involved in ensuring e-learning becomes an important facet of mainstream teaching and learning practice. We hope this book will help you develop ideas for your own practice. The web site for this series is connecting-with-elearning.com.

Allison Littlejohn and Chris Pegler (series editors), January 2007

Acknowledgements

Many friends and colleagues at The Open University, the University of Auckland and the University of Strathclyde have contributed to the development of this book. In particular we wish to thank the Open University course team responsible for 'The eLearning Professional' for helping to refine our ideas about e-portfolios and Professor Kathy Kane and Ian Thompson at the University of Strathclyde for introducing us to SPIDER.

The authors also wish to acknowledge the significant contribution of Raewyn Heays (New Zealand) and Steve Davies (UK) in commenting on and proofreading drafts, and offering support and encouragement throughout the production process. On a more personal front, we thank Frances Devaney and Rhys Pegler Davies for their keen interest, support and patience.

Finally, there would have been no book without Allison Littlejohn (Glasgow Caledonian University) who had the idea of including this book in the new Connecting with e-Learning series. Thanks Allison!

List of abbreviations

ADA	Americans with Disabilities Act
BBC	British Broadcasting Corporation
BECTA	British Educational Communications and Technology Agency
CATS	Creating Accessible Teaching and Support programme
CPD	Continuing professional development
CMS	Content management system
CSCL	Computer supported collaborative learning
CV	Curriculum vitae (resume)
DDA	Disability Discrimination Act
DDP	Diagnostic Digital Portfolio (Alverno College)
DfES	Department for Education and Skills
EAL	English as an additional language
EHE	Enterprise in Higher Education
ELE	Electronic learning environment
e-PDP	e-Personal development portfolio
EPICC	European Initiatives Co-ordination Committee
FE	Further Education
HE	Higher Education
HEFCE	Higher Education Funding Council for England
HESA	Higher Education Statistics Agency
HTML	Hypertext mark-up language
ICT	Information and communications technologies
IMS	IMS Global Learning Consortium
IT	Information Technology
JISC	Joint Information Systems Committee
LO	Learning object
LP	Learning information profile (IMS)
ME	Myalgic Encephalopathy

MERLOT	Multimedia Educational Resource for Learning and Online Teaching
MP3	MPEG-1 Audio Layer 3
MSN	The Microsoft Network
NECC	National Education Computing Conference
NITLE	National Institute for Technology and Liberal Education
OSP	Open source portfolios
OSPI	Open Source Portfolio Initiative
OU	UK Open University
pdf	Portable Document Format (Adobe)
PDP	Personal development plan
PEP	Personal education plan
PETAL	Personal e-portfolios for teaching and learning project
QAA	Quality Assurance Agency (for Higher Education)
QCA	Qualifications and Curriculum Authority
RSS	Really Simple Syndication
SAFARI	Skills in accessing, finding and reviewing information project
SCIL	Stanford Center for Innovations in Learning
SIESWE	Scottish Institute for Excellence in Social Work Education
SLU	St Lawrence University
SOAP	Simple Object Access Protocol
SPIDER	Strathclyde Personal, Interactive, Development and Educational Resource
tml	Tutorial markup language
UCAS	Universities and Colleges Admissions System
URL	Unique resource locator
SCIL	Stanford Center for Innovations in Learning
VETP	Vocational Educational and Training Programme (Denmark)
VLE	Virtual learning environment
VTeP	Virginia Tech ePortfolio
WAI	Web Accessibility Initiative
WYSIWYG	What you see is what you get
ZU	Zayed University

Introduction

This book has been a learning journey for each of its authors. We started that journey by delving into the existing research on e-portfolios. We emerged after over a year, somewhat frustrated. Useful and comprehensive volumes such as Jafari and Kaufman's *Handbook of Research on ePortfolios* (Jafari and Kaufman, 2006) had only just been published as our own book was going to press. It sometimes seems that the e-portfolio landscape is changing and coming into (and out of) focus week by week. We recognise that there will be important research on e-portfolios as their adoption becomes more widespread. Research from which we will all learn a great deal. Unfortunately we cannot wait for this and, if you are interested in this book, you may also be unable to wait for all the answers to emerge. There is considerable interest in e-portfolios and we know that college and university staff need something to help them to identify and think through the issues now.

In producing this book, we wanted to write something which would be useful and interesting to practitioners, a text which spoke from experience and evidence. Again we encountered obstacles. For many months we seemed to be constantly questioning ourselves, often doubting ourselves. Was there enough – yet – known about e-portfolios? We could see their potential, but where was the evidence for their use? What were the experiences that we would draw on?

We have written a book which blends reference to e-portfolio research and experience to date. We have drawn cases from further and higher education and from several countries. We have also 'borrowed', in so far as this was useful, from the world of paper-based portfolios. Throughout this book we have looked at the range of purposes to which an e-portfolio may be put – as showcase, development tool, assessment approach, or resource for reflection. We have considered national examples of e-portfolios as well as institutional, departmental and course-specific implementations. We are writing this book at a time when there is still a great deal unknown about e-portfolios, but we have nonetheless looked to the future. This might appear to be a risky venture, but we have tried to provide some guidance on what you might expect from e-portfolios. We have approached this in two ways. First, by looking at some of the newer learning technologies (blogs, wikis and podcasts) which already shed some light on the possible future form and use of e-portfolios. Then, we looked beyond the known or highly predictable, to offer some scenarios for e-portfolio use across a range of contexts, some of which may surprise you.

As befits a book in an e-learning series this one was developed online without the three authors meeting face-to-face. Professor Lorraine Stefani is based at the University of Auckland in New Zealand and Professor Robin Mason and Chris Pegler at The Open University in the UK. The authors have not yet met in person, but the online working relationship has been intense, productive and rewarding.

Effective online collaborations such as ours point to what we might expect from online sharing amongst our students. The internet offers phenomenal potential for publishing and discussing experiences, and learning together. This is what we have done in this venture. We have learned together. It is also something that we expect from e-portfolios, the openness to sharing, working with others online, and producing an improved 'product' through reflection and development.

We have emerged with our confidence in e-portfolios renewed. They *do* offer a very different approach to supporting teaching and learning, one which has the potential to be transformational for colleges and universities. It is hardly surprising that interest is gathering momentum at a time when e-portfolios offer a very good 'fit' with some of the other changes within further and higher education. We can see the resonance with themes of personalisation, widening participation, workplace learning, authentic assessment and personal development planning.

Each of the chapters within this book considers the wider implications of e-portfolio use. Throughout the book we also consider the implications of e-portfolio implementation for students, staff and the institution. Without clear commitment from all three, e-portfolio initiatives cannot achieve their full potential. Some e-portfolio initiatives will fail in this respect. Staff will constrain the implementation, institutions will take control and students will at best conform or comply with their use. This will for these implementations be a lost opportunity. There are now enough early adopters to indicate the potential of e-portfolios. They can have a profound and beneficial impact on students, staff and institution.

Below we give a brief description of each chapter. Although we have structured the book so that it could be read in sequence, some of these topics may be of greater – more immediate – interest to you. Dipping into particular chapters without reading the preceding ones should not present a problem for the reader. Any technical or unfamiliar terms are covered in the Glossary at the end of the book. We have also provided a list of useful websites at the end of each chapter. These lists and others are also linked to the *Connecting with e-Learning series* website.

In Chapter 1 we start by locating e-portfolios within e-learning more generally and then move on to consider various definitions of what an e-portfolio is, and the variety of ways in which they are applied. Here we also identify some of the big issues that we return to in later chapters. We conclude by highlighting significant environmental changes in standards and software, policy drivers and convergence.

The significance of e-portfolios is expanded on further in Chapter 2. We start by looking at some of the distinct differences in functionality and opportunity which e-portfolios present. The chapter then goes on to relate the rise in interest in e-portfolios to the increased emphasis on reflective lifelong learning, and in particular the emergence of the personal development portfolio. Throughout this chapter we draw on work with paper-based portfolios to better understand what the purpose of the e-portfolio is likely to be, and how its use could be embedded into the curriculum. Examples from the UK and US are used to consider department-level and institutional implementations.

Chapter 3 provides an exploration of the issues which we need to consider when we think about implementing e-portfolios, at course, programme, departmental or institutional level. It touches on both the advantages and disadvantages of moving to e-portfolios and identifies six specific issues relating to the early stages of e-portfolio adoption and discussion. There is particular emphasis on clarifying the *purpose* of the e-portfolio, whether this is focused on showcase, assessment, development or reflection, or some blend of these. The scope of the implementation is also considered, looking at some of the operational questions that you will need to address. The chapter finishes by considering whether the level of e-learning maturity within your own organisation would support e-portfolio implementation.

Course design is the focus of Chapter 4. We take seriously the point made by Ehrmann (Erhmann, 2004) that e-portfolios will not in themselves create a 'magical' improvement in education. The e-portfolio needs to work within an appropriate course design. What course designs will be most suitable? How will the e-portfolio impact on course design?

This chapter takes us beyond the simple repository (storehouse) model of an e-portfolio into considering how e-portfolio use can bring about curriculum changes. We also start to consider the role of assessment, a subject that is explored in more detail in Chapter 5.

Chapter 5 continues and expands on the role of e-portfolios in assessment. It looks in particular at constructivist and authentic learning approaches and also at peer and self-assessment. Changes in assessment are considered, including a de-emphasis on reliability. We look at the different roles of the e-portfolio in formative and summative assessment, and the problems in using developmental and reflective e-portfolios for assessment. These tensions were identified in Chapter 4 and are considered in more depth here. Also in this chapter we consider some models for how to assess e-portfolios, but also highlight some dilemmas in using e-portfolios for assessment.

Returning to the diverse definitions of e-portfolios and their applications, we use Chapter 6 to explore in detail the role of the e-portfolio as a tool for professional development. We consider here developments in e-teaching portfolios and the opportunities that an electronic format offers. We explore in detail an example drawn from a New Zealand university, considering in depth the implications of this pilot for practitioners and staff developers.

Another sort of opportunity arising from e-portfolios is explored in Chapter 7. Here we consider the implications of e-portfolios for inclusive learning. In part this is a discussion about the inclusiveness of any online learning, but there are specific accessibility issues around the use of e-portfolios. We explore how implementation of e-portfolios can be made accessible, taking the example of dyslexia to show how we might need to approach implementation. While use of multiple media is one of the strengths of e-portfolio use, and can be enabling to some students, it can be disabling to others. Also we note here that disability may affect staff and employers as well as students. It really is an issue for everyone.

There is no doubt that e-portfolios are technically a complex problem. When we think about the advantages of e-portfolio use across institutions as part of lifelong learning we are taking for granted that there will be no problems of interoperability. But how realistic is this? Chapter 8 focuses on current thinking as it relates to e-portfolio systems, and in particular the influential IMS e-portfolio specification and the issue of standards. We consider some of the options in system choice – commercial systems, systems developed in-house, and open source alternatives. We then look at an example of an electronic personal development portfolio at Strathclyde University, using SPIDER.

In the last two chapters of the book we turn to the question of the future. We can see that the potential of e-portfolios is all in front of us. What will e-portfolio use be like when it has achieved scale, is widely accepted and is making full use of the technology? These are difficult questions to answer. In Chapter 9 we look at three technologies which have only recently been assimilated into education. Blogs, wikis and podcasts can all be included as elements within an e-portfolio, but more importantly they can all offer some insights into how students may use technology with these kinds of features. By exploring these new technologies we can make certain assumptions about how e-portfolios might be used.

In the final chapter we look further into the future and present six very different scenarios for e-portfolio use. We have not strayed so far that these are incredible science fiction. Each case is very credible, but some of the implications that we identify may nonetheless be unexpected. From the college leaver trying to make an impression on an employer, to the grandmother who is creating an heirloom for future generations, we consider what purpose e-portfolios might play if their use became universal. We also note some of the problems that may arise as a result. Won't it be interesting to see which of our hopes, and fears, are realised?

Our aim has been to provide a book which identifies and explores the issues around e-portfolio implementation as well as looking forward to what they may bring. The decision as to whether to use e-portfolios is not one which should be taken lightly. The real potential for students, staff and institutions will come from general and widespread use so that the skills become commonplace and the technology ubiquitous. This could be a beneficial learning and teaching tool across all discipline areas, not just those which have a history of portfolio use. However, we also need to recognise that some institutions will be unprepared to adopt e-portfolios at this stage. Some staff will be unprepared to support them. Many students – no matter how ICT-literate – will need preparation if they are to understand what an e-portfolio is for. We hope that this book will help you understand whether you are ready to take the step towards e-portfolio implementation. It should certainly help you to contribute to informed discussion on this topic.

Chapter 1

E-portfolios and e-learning

It is hazardous writing a book about a practice – the use of e-portfolios – when its development is in such an early stage. E-portfolios might evolve into something unrecognisable today or they might become yesterday's unsuccessful idea. Yet this is the very point at which potential adopters are most interested in deciding whether the practice has anything to offer them. Fortunately most people who work with new technologies are used to the way in which the language, the tools and the practice change very rapidly. This will undoubtedly be the case with e-portfolios.

It was certainly the case with e-learning which has passed from a niche practice for distance learners to a mainstream activity in face-to-face education at all levels. As practice has evolved, the language to describe it has moved from 'computer conferencing' and 'online learning' to 'distributed education' and 'blended learning'. The tools have become richer as well: synchronous and asynchronous modes of interaction, webliographies and e-journals, podcasting and blogging. E-portfolios at one level are another tool in the e-learning armoury. They address many of the same issues: lifelong and personalised learning, flexible and student-centred pedagogies, web-based teaching and new forms of assessment. At another level e-portfolios are, or might become, more significant than e-learning. If we drop the 'e' from both of these terms, as many practitioners recommend, we are left with learning and portfolios. These are the key concepts; digitising them is simply the reflection of other technology trends and developments.

It has been argued that online connectivity is transforming the practice of learning (Rennie and Mason, 2004), though this transformation is often in spite of rather than because of the nature of the teaching. It is apparent that the extraordinary take-up of mobile phones and iPods and the explosive growth of practices such as blogging and texting have been user-driven. They have been socially engineered rather than educationally or institutionally engineered. Teachers and course designers are now beginning to integrate these technologies and practices into formal education because they are so popular with young people, not because their educational value was always recognised.

If portfolios were to suddenly 'take off' and become the new 'must-have' social gizmo, the implications would be immense. In this imaginary scenario, everyone would have a personal online space where they would store their 'life's work' and make presentations of it in different formats for an array of different audiences: friends and family, school and higher education, workmates and job interviews. It would be a repository for all their accomplishments, their hopes and their reflections. It would stay with them for life and be a constant updatable companion: a diary, a CV, a record, a forward planner. Fanciful? Perhaps, but that is the 'promise' of e-portfolios in the long term.

At the moment, the development of e-portfolios is caught in a dilemma: the imaginary scenario or even a mundane scenario of students having a portfolio throughout their college or university career, needs the user to feel ownership of the portfolio in order to have any chance of success. Like their mobile phone or their iPod, their portfolio must 'be with them' all the time. However, for a portfolio to be useful it needs to integrate with many other systems and institutions so that vital information can be transferred (e.g. their school record, course details and marks) and the software can be interoperable and 'future-proof'. Current practice, as this book will demonstrate, pays lip-service to student ownership, but remains largely teacher and institution led. The technology is still immature; the uses are still fluctuating and even the definitions, the concept of what an e-portfolio is, are hugely varied.

E-portfolios defined

As this book is primarily for educators, the e-portfolio definitions we consider arise from an e-learning context, though we are aware that broader perspectives are possible. One example of the shifting nature of e-portfolio development is that the very term 'e-portfolio' is sometimes used to refer to:

1   the software
2   a particular presentation of material
3   all of the content from which a particular presentation is selected.

Furthermore, there is evidence in current literature that for some users and developers, an e-portfolio system is virtually synonymous with an electronic learning environment (ELE), whereas for others it is something much more contained, individual and limited in facilities.

The following definitions give a flavour of current opinions:

> Portfolios, in education and personal or professional development, are collections of documents and other objects that can be shown as evidence to support claims a person makes about what they know, what they have achieved, and what they can do. As for e-portfolios, a common starting point is that they are simply electronic versions of physical portfolios that contain digital objects instead of physical objects. They are, '... the new generation of the old 3-ring binder'. (http://www.jisc.ac.uk/media/documents/programmes/distributed_e learning/myworld_petal2_draftfinal.doc)

Penn State University was one of the early adopters of e-portfolio approaches, and their site is full of useful resources. Interestingly, at Penn State the use of e-portfolios developed from the use of personal web pages.

Their definition is: e-portfolios are, '... personalized, web-based collections that include ... reflective annotations and commentary related to these experiences' (http://eportfolio.psu.edu/about/index. html).

A broader definition or description is:

> A system which allows users to record any abilities, events or plans which are personally significant; which allows these records to be linked, augmented or evidenced by other data sources, and which promotes reflection on these entries. It allows the user to integrate institutional data with personal data, recorded and reviewed over time, which has been enriched by commentary and feedback from the recipients of shared assets. It is a system with tools for aggregating assets in multiple forms; for telling myriad stories to diverse audiences and which provides absolute user-control over what is shared, with whom, for what purpose and for how long. It is a personal repository; a personal diary; a feedback and collaboration system; and a digital theatre – where the audience is by invitation only.
>
> Pebblepad (http://www.pebblepad.co.uk/dev2/ viewasset.aspx?oid=1868&type=thought)

Finally, a more extensive learning-based definition:

- a repository of information about a particular learner provided by the learner and by other people and organisations, including products in a range of media that the learner has created or helped to create alongside formal documents from authoritative sources, such as transcripts of assessed achievement, which the learner has chosen to retain
- principally owned by the learner, although some of the things it contains may be co-owned, for example an individual learning plan containing past results and future targets negotiated between learner and teacher, or fully owned by another party, for example a showcase set of architectural drawings for a client
- capable of providing the information about a learner from which different profiles of the learner may be developed through other services and retained within the e-portfolio
- typically provided by an organisation which may set conditions for its use. An individual may have a single e-portfolio or a sequence of e-portfolios and may make simultaneous use of several e-portfolios. An e-portfolio for Lifelong Learning is the aggregation of all an individual's e-portfolios such that they appear to the owner as a seamless whole.

(http://www.elframework.org/learning_domain_
services/eportfolio/forums/public/563531763371)

From these definitions a number of issues arise:

- Ownership
- Multimedia components
- Reflection
- Evidence
- Multiple presentations.

It is also evident that there are different uses for e-portfolios. Table 1.1 provides some examples of applications of e-portfolios.

Relating to e-learning

E-portfolios are used by students at traditional universities and colleges where face-to-face teaching is the dominant mode of teaching. They are also used in distributed, blended and totally online learning programmes

Table 1.1 Applications of e-portfolios

E-portfolio types	Explanation
Course portfolio	Portfolios assembled by students for one course. They document and reflect upon the ways in which the student has met the outcomes for that particular course. Course portfolios are often used for part or all of the course assessment.
Programme portfolio	Portfolios that students develop to document the work they have completed, the skills they have learned, and the outcomes they have met in an academic department or programme. It could be a requirement for graduation. Students might use a selection from their programme portfolio to show to prospective employers.
Institutional portfolio	This kind of portfolio is a personal development planning tool, in which each employee records achievements, future plans and extra-curricular activities. The mentor or appraiser could add comments.

and institutions. Whatever the primary focus of engagement with students, the use of e-portfolios inevitably adds a strong online element to the teaching and learning. Institutions need to provide electronic support and services; teachers need access and skills to integrate the e-portfolio application into their overall course design, and students need a wide range of electronic abilities in order to develop their e-portfolio.

The underlying pedagogy of e-portfolio use is probably the most significant link with e-learning however. As e-learning is the focus of much experimentation across a wide variety of disciplines and levels, it is perhaps too early to talk about an underlying theory to which the majority of researchers would subscribe. Nevertheless, constructivism does seem to be the approach most commonly evident in e-learning courses. Bangert supports this view: 'The majority of the Web-based courses today are designed using constructivist educational principles' (Bangert, 2004).

In the constructivist theory the emphasis is placed on the learner or the student rather than the teacher or the instructor. It is the learner who interacts with content and events and thereby gains an understanding of the ideas or events. The learner, therefore, constructs his/her own conceptualisations and solutions to problems. Learner autonomy and initiative are not only accepted but actively encouraged. Furthermore, the process of discussion, reading other learners' messages and receiving feedback on one's own messages, provides the environment and scaffolding necessary for higher-order thinking (Slavin, 1994). Constructivist theory claims that this kind of thinking depends to some extent on a socio-cultural and communicative experience (Stacey, 1998).

The aim of constructivist principles as applied to e-learning is to engender independent, self-reliant learners who have the confidence and skill to use a range of strategies to construct their own knowledge. Eklund *et al.* writing for the Australian Flexible Learning Framework, note: 'The attainment of higher-order knowledge, attitudes and approaches embedded in a social context and made all the more possible through technology is an aim of education in the post-modern society' (Eklund *et al.* 2003).

Where students are required to develop and maintain an e-portfolio, they are usually expected to reflect on their learning, consider how to give evidence of their learning and possibly even develop a plan of what they would like to learn. In short, an e-portfolio implementation usually implies a considerable level of learner autonomy and initiative, of learner responsibility for their learning and of opportunities to refine their learning based on feedback from the teacher.

As with e-learning in general, many students resist teachers' efforts to pass responsibility for learning onto each individual learner. In some e-portfolio implementations, students spend their time making multimedia gimmicks which do not demonstrate their learning. They do not take the initiative in maintaining and updating their e-portfolio. As Chapter 4 concludes, weaker students especially need considerable support and scaffolding in order to become self-directed. This applies to many other e-learning applications, as well as to e-portfolio uses.

Institutional engagement

There are a range of generic services which institutions using e-learning need to provide. Many of these are required for e-portfolio use as well. Assessment processes are usually key to both – for example, systems for submitting assignments electronically, for marking and commenting and providing electronic transcripts. Systems are needed for ensuring security, privacy, ownership and authentication. Training is required for both staff and students in whatever software is chosen.

The vision of an e-portfolio as a lifelong learning tool that is updated throughout life has considerable institutional implications. Are colleges and universities expected to continue hosting the e-portfolios of all their past students? Can one tool encompass the myriad uses of a lifelong e-portfolio, one that contains authenticated transcripts, reflections and memorabilia, and multimedia items such as audio and video clips, one that stores and presents, one that is learner-centred, but institutionally hosted? There is an interesting parallel here with the early applications of online learning. When distance learning students first had the opportunity of interacting online with their fellow students, some wanted this facility to continue after the end of their course or programme. Providing lifelong access to online discussion forums would be completely unreasonable, but some universities have developed alumni access sites in order to continue allegiance with the institution and hopefully attract them back for further study.

Just as there are institutional benefits to e-learning, so there are with e-portfolios. For example, e-portfolio use can be the basis for:

- Creating a system of tracking student work over time, in a single course, with students and faculty reflecting on it
- Having a more fully informed and dynamic, constantly updated view of student progress in a program, which is very helpful in formative assessment
- Aggregating many students' work in a particular course to see how the students as a whole are progressing toward learning goals
- Assessing many courses in similar ways that are all part of one major and thus, by extension, assessing the entire program of study.

(Batson, 2005)

Institutional benefits from e-learning include the ability to address the widening participation agenda, the need to provide greater flexibility for students who have part-time jobs and the opportunity to contact staff and students electronically, in short, e-administration.

E-portfolios as e-learning

E-portfolios are being used to meet a range of different learning requirements. The following list may be extended as developments occur:

1 *Assessment* – used to demonstrate achievement against some criteria.
2 *Presentation* – used to evidence learning in a persuasive way, often related to professional qualifications.
3 *Learning* – used to document, guide and advance learning over time.

4   *Personal development* – related to professional development and employment.
5   *Multiple owner* – allow more than one person to participate in development of content.
6   *Working* – combine previous types, with one or more e-portfolios and also a wider archive to provide evidence of learning at work.

The distinction between these uses is not clear-cut and most colleges and universities would probably want an e-portfolio system which offered all of these functions. The teaching and administrative staff might want their own portfolio as use spreads and is integrated with existing staff development processes.

Standards

The history of e-learning development is marked by the need for standards in order to ensure interoperability, security and usability. These needs are also hallmarks of e-portfolios, especially as we contemplate a lifelong learning e-portfolio.

There are two aspects of interoperability – one is the passing of data such as marks from the central system to the individual e-portfolio; the other is the 'dream' of moving one's personal e-portfolio from one system to another, from school, to college, to the workplace.
Developing this level of interoperability will depend on the growth and take-up of e-portfolios and the consequent demand, just as the telephone network needs to be globally interoperable.

Studies have already been carried out and reports written on the legal and records management issues relating to lifelong learner records and e-portfolio systems (www.jiscinfonet.ac.uk/InfoKits/effective-use-of-VLEs/e-portfolios).

Software

In the early days of e-learning, many universities developed their own electronic 'learning environments' (though this is a more recent term). Some universities are still soldiering on with their home-grown products. The advent of electronic learning environments, such as WebCT and Blackboard, met the demand from smaller universities and colleges for an 'off the shelf' solution requiring less technical expertise and greater functionality for teaching staff to input their own content. At least one of these, WebCT, was an offshoot of a system designed in a university.

Currently e-portfolio development is undergoing the same journey. A number of early adopter universities have developed their own e-portfolio systems – for example, the University of Wolverhampton which has developed an e-portfolio they call PebblePad. Similarly e-portfolio tools are being developed and trialled in departments and different subjects contexts. Commercial systems and open source e-portfolios have also been developed as Chapter 8 describes. No front-runner has yet emerged, but this will undoubtedly change in time.

Meantime, a new generation of technology is already in development in the UK whereby an e-portfolio for lifelong learning will no longer be an institution-provided package or system. It will be a learner-owned application, independent of any individual institution, interacting with services accessed over the web. This initiative is being led by The Joint Information Systems Committee (JISC). (www.jisc.ac.uk/mle_lifelong-glearning_info.html).

Policy drivers

E-learning, once it emerged from the shadows of distance learning, began to become the focus of government and institutional policies. Not to have an e-learning policy as few as five years ago, was a serious oversight on the part of any college or university in the UK. National policies and funding also provided a significant impetus to the development and spread of e-learning. The same is true for e-portfolios.

In 2005 the UK-based Department for Education and Skills (DfES) *e-Strategy, Harnessing Technology: Transforming learning and children's services,* proposed a personal online learning space for every learner, which contributes to an electronic portfolio to build a record of achievement throughout lifelong learning (www.dfes.gov.uk/publications /e-strategy). At higher education level, The Higher Education Funding Council for England (HEFCE) produced a strategy for e-learning which included an objective to encourage electronic support for describing learning achievement and personal development planning. It also directed two other national UK bodies, The Joint Information Systems Committee (JISC) and the Higher Education Academy (HEA) to investigate the use of e-portfolios across institutions and sectors (www.hefce. ac.uk/Pubs/hefce/2005/05_12/).

In 2004, the Qualifications and Curriculum Authority (QCA) *Blueprint for e-Assessment* proposed that by 2009 all awarding bodies should be set up to accept and assess e-portfolios. Likewise the UK system for university admissions, UCAS, has committed itself to moving to entirely web-based admissions and review processes.

These policy drivers represent a significant pressure for colleges and universities to engage with e-portfolio developments, as e-administration, e-admissions and e-learning become standard practice.

Convergence

One of the distinguishing trends in e-learning is that of convergence. ELEs represented the convergence of asynchronous communication with web-based course content and online resources. Currently we are witnessing the convergence of blogging and podcasting (see Chapter 9), both in terms of software and of applications. E-portfolios for some users and developers have already become another 'button' in a virtual learning environment (VLE); the reflective components of e-portfolios have great similarities with blogging; the commenting facilities of e-portfolios replicate the function of asynchronous conferencing; the assessment function of e-portfolios replicate to some extent the facilities of most VLEs. A personal webpage carries many of the presentational functions of e-portfolios. Consequently, e-portfolios are a composite of facilities and functions that already exist in other types of software. Any claim to be something unique would rest on very shaky ground.

On the one hand this composite quality of e-portfolios should be reassuring to teachers: we are not facing a new phenomenon which we must master and try to apply to education, as arguably was the case for blogging and podcasting. On the other hand, if it is not new, then why bother to engage with it? Can the same benefits be had from using all the separate elements already existing in other forms – the VLE, blogging, personal webpages and online assignments? The answer in some cases may be yes, but our experience of other disparate functions brought together is that there are major gains in usability, in motivation and in opportunities to rethink current practice. This continues to be the case with e-learning, namely, that many of the significant gains in student learning come from the disruptive nature of the process which 'encourages' teachers to analyse their existing approaches to teaching and design new ones for the functions e-learning offers. E-portfolios may well be the tipping point that e-learning really needs to be a fully functioning approach to learning without the 'e'!

Chapter 2

The e-portfolio as a tool for learning

As Chapter 1 showed, there are many definitions of an electronic portfolio. They vary according to the context in which the portfolio is used and the uses for which it is intended. In this chapter we focus on the use of e-portfolios within college and university settings. We are defining electronic portfolios in these contexts as digitised collections of student work and reflections. These could be assembled in websites, electronic learning environments (ELE), or copied onto recorded media such as CD-ROM, DVDs. In some cases there will be use of tailor-made e-portfolio software (e.g. ePortaro).

There are three obvious differences between the e-portfolio and the paper based folio:

- With a digital portfolio, *it is easy to rearrange, edit and combine materials.* The student can determine an order of storage, but then vary that order according to the requirements of the moment. They can search on and access content in a non-linear fashion. They can make modifications on a regular basis to suit their needs and the expectations and requirements of different audiences. For example a tutor and a prospective employer/interviewer will have different expectations of the portfolio. In digital form it can be edited and collated to suit these different needs, including offering variety in layouts or appearance of the same content.

- *The e-portfolio is a 'connected document'.* The student can use hyperlinking to connect documents together, linking between the portfolio elements and also to external sources and references. It is easier to make obvious a range of associations between different subject areas, learning experiences or observations, content and other artefacts (Yancey, 2001).

- *There is portability to the e-portfolio which does not exist without the electronic form.* The classic image of a physically unwieldy portfolio, almost overburdening the student, is replaced by a set of digital files which can be transported and transferred with ease. The e-portfolio can be accessed and used in a variety of locations and can be replicated and shared with others. It is portable and mobile.

Over the course of a student's life the e-portfolio will need to play a variety of roles. The ease with which the digital form can be adapted, linked and transported is key to the emergence of new ways of using the idea of a portfolio. One of the uses of e-portfolios which most closely resembles the use of physical portfolios is as a digitised showcase of student work and skills. Often the purpose is to present student work to prospective employers, to secure investment funding, or to obtain a place on a postgraduate course. The analogy here is generally with an artist's portfolio. This is a collection of the highest quality work that the student is capable of, and typically shows the range of work, perhaps with an idea of progression over time. It is a showcase of the student's versatility and an indicator of their potential. In this sense an electronic format offers greater potential for a larger range of students. The work of performing artists, engineers, doctors or accountants could all be very effectively displayed in an e-portfolio, using multimedia. Students entering these professions would struggle to assemble useful non-digital, portable showcases for their skills.

As well as providing a means of presenting evidence of learning and achievement, the e-portfolio can be a reflective document spanning the student's development and helping learners to become critical thinkers. This idea is often linked to the idea of a portfolio as a 'personal development plan' (PDP). It can aid the development of the student's writing and communication skills. It can also support the development of information and technology literacy skills, including skills in productive use of multimedia (Lorenzo and Ittelson, 2005).

The e-portfolio offers several interesting advantages just by virtue of its digital form and the rise in systems to exploit that. However, on its own, it is unlikely to transform learning. It is a tool, around which we may wish to modify our teaching. To understand why and how we might do this we really need to see examples of the e-portfolio being incorporated into the learning context.

Setting the stage for e-portfolio development

Many people writing about e-portfolios believe that the benefit of e-portfolios has more to do with the active process of e-portfolio development than with the portfolio product itself. They see the development of the e-portfolio *over time* as key. The emphasis is on the development process and what this offers the student, rather than on a polished end product, no matter how versatile. This view proposes that the real relevance of an e-portfolio is in working document form, charting work-in-progress, work accomplished, and future plans of work.

Di Biase *et al.* (2002) offer a view of the development of a portfolio from simple collection of materials, through selection, reflection and projection to final presentation. They emphasise the value of each of the stages, giving a 'feel' for the purpose of the portfolio, an idea of how it links with learning:

1 *Collection of materials* – students, with support from teachers, save artefacts (assignments, presentations) that represent achievements, successes (and positive development opportunities) in their day-to-day study.

2 *Selection of materials* – students review and evaluate potential portfolio material to identify those that demonstrate the development of particular skills or achievement of specific standards.

3 *Reflection* – students evaluate or assess their own learning through reflective commentary. They reflect on their own growth and development over time, recognising achievement of goals and standards, identifying gaps in development or understanding and acknowledging skills requiring further work.

4 *Projection (or Direction)* – students, with the teacher's assistance, compare current achievements or outcomes to standards or performance indicators. They then set learning goals or develop action plans for the future. This stage links portfolio development and personal development planning (PDP) to support lifelong learning.

5 *Presentation* – students are invited to share their portfolio with teachers and possibly their peers. This promotes collaborative learning, fosters self and peer evaluation and further encourages commitment to PDP and lifelong learning.

This sense of progress through stages gives some indication that the act of compiling a portfolio with a focus on *presentation* does not in itself guarantee that active learning and reflection will occur. If the e-portfolio is to become a tool to support active learning, it has to be promoted as such. A teacher trying to introduce the use of e-portfolios as other than a simple showcase must empathise with the range of stages and purposes. Their introduction needs to cover the development of the e-portfolio from simple collection to final presentation, so that students fully understand the nature of the commitment and what is expected of them. While high achievers in college and university may see the benefits immediately, weaker and less confident students may think of an e-portfolio as simply a collection of learning materials. Students approaching their use of e-portfolios with low expectations will take longer to grasp the concepts of reflection and personal development planning.

Linking e-portfolios and reflective lifelong learning

The phrases 'lifelong learning', 'personal development planning' and 'learning portfolios' all came into being at approximately the same time. It is probably not surprising therefore that there are obvious connections between them. Successful lifelong learning implies that citizens be provided with learning opportunities at all ages and in numerous contexts. It assumes that learners will need to continue to learn throughout their lives. Their learning environment and their motive for learning will both vary over time. Learners could be learning at and for work, at home, and through leisure activities. They could be learning through being part of a community. Most of this learning will not be through formal channels such as school, college or university.

The reasons given for emphasis on lifelong learning often stem from the demands of the workplace. Despite the increased duration of primary, secondary and tertiary education, the knowledge and skills acquired through formal education are unlikely to be sufficient for jobs or careers spanning three or four decades. The acceleration of scientific and technological progress has led to demands for re-skilling of previously well-qualified workers. However, the emphasis is not, or should not be, wholly on acquisition of new skills in formal educational settings. Lifelong learning is attitudinal in nature and requires that one can and should be open to new ideas, decisions, skills or behaviours.

In the UK, there has been a strong push by the Quality Assurance Agency (QAA) for Higher Education for the integration of PDP into the curriculum. The QAA has strongly encouraged the implementation of portfolios to support students in their understanding and ownership of the personal development processes.

Personal Development Planning is defined as:

> A structured and supported process undertaken by individuals to reflect upon their own learning performance and or achievement and to plan for their personal, educational and career development.
>
> (QAA, 2001)

If learners begin to understand the ideas behind PDP and recognise that learning doesn't end when they finish college or university, the processes of PDP should stand them in good stead to become lifelong learners in the widest sense.

A good example of linking lifelong learning, PDP and portfolios comes from the Danish Ministry of Education and its Vocational Education and Training Programme (VETP). The Danish Ministry has promoted the importance of students being actively involved and engaged in their learning experiences. One major innovation is the personal education plan (PEP) and the educational portfolio or 'log book'. The PEP and the portfolio or log book are seen as complementary. They put the emphasis on students taking responsibility for their own learning. All students enrolled in vocational education and training have their own personal education plan. The point of the log book or portfolio is to help them to record and reflect on their learning.

For many years vocational educators have favoured practical demonstrations of knowledge and competence (Little, 1992). Vocational educators are necessarily concerned with preparing students for the expectations of the workplace. However employers are increasingly emphasising the importance of 'softer' skills. As Yorke and Knight (2004) point out, employers increasingly want to appoint staff who can demonstrate critical thinking, teamwork, self-evaluation/assessment skills, adaptability and flexibility. Employers want to see *evidence* of these skills. The challenge for students and their teachers is how can development of these skills be demonstrated for employers?

Some vocational educators see the e-portfolio as an obvious route to collating and displaying documentation and presenting multiple, tangible forms of evidence. The electronic portfolio can support a wider variety of evidence in formats that allow clearer demonstration of some of the softer skills. It offers further convenience for job search in providing evidence in a format that is more easily transferable, and more portable.

Some colleges and universities in the USA have been developing the e-portfolio concept over a substantial period of time. For example, the

Stanford Center for Innovations in Learning (SCIL) has been exploring the use of electronic learning portfolios in higher education since 1998. Much of the thinking behind the SCIL portfolio projects is based on the changing nature of student lives and the increased level of competition associated with the job market. The SCIL e-portfolio recognises that students are involved in work placements, or working to support themselves through college or university. Students' informal learning in these contexts may include valuable experiences which complement and supplement those designated in their formal course or curriculum. The e-portfolio can thus offer a beneficially holistic view of the student's development and a more accurate presentation of the range of their abilities. As Chen *et al.* (2002) have pointed out, students are now required to be both creative and resilient. Innovative and flexible tools and practices are necessary in order to support the changing needs of today's learners.

In the UK, the idea of learning portfolios gained ground in the early 1990s partly as a result of the Department for Employment and Skills (now the DfES) Enterprise in Higher Education (UK) initiative (EHE). The emphasis of the EHE initiative was on:

- active learning
- the development of transferable skills
- enhancing the relevance of the curriculum to the world of work
- a requirement for graduates to be flexible and adaptable in accordance with the changing nature of the workplace
- promoting an understanding of learning and a recognition of the skills and attributes associated with lifelong learning.

This focus on the changing nature of the curriculum recognised that passive learning, knowledge transmission and regurgitation of course content for the purposes of assessment was not adequate. It could not encourage the development of reflective, self-aware and self-critical learners. But how easy is it to do this? Can e-portfolios help students in discussing and developing their conceptions of 'reflection', 'critical analysis' and self-assessment?

Paper-based e-portfolio prototypes

Notwithstanding the early e-portfolio experiences at Stanford and other US institutions, most colleges and universities have not, until now, been equipped to generate or handle e-portfolios. There is little sustained experience of e-portfolio use to draw on. However, progress in explaining the potential of e-portfolios can be made through examination of paper-based portfolios. Paper-based portfolios to some extent presage future use of e-portfolios.

The UK Open University was particularly keen to capitalise on the potential of the Enterprise in Higher Education initiative. With 220,000 mature students, many already in employment, it gained funding to develop the 'A Portfolio Approach to Personal and Career Development' course. Targeted at students studying for a higher level educational qualification, this course broke new ground by providing the 'self-assessment' and self-development material as well as a portfolio to record learning achievements. It also developed an enhanced staff development programme to support this project, and forged national and regional partnerships with employers to make use of the portfolio (Maher, 2001).

As was common with EHE projects, the underlying principle of this Open University course was the learning process rather than course content. This was in keeping with the ideals of 'lifelong learning' and 'student-centred learning' established within the project and within this institution. The project encouraged students to take responsibility for their own learning, This was possibly one of the first initiatives in the UK to emphasise, value, and credit 'the learning process' – through a portfolio of learning evidence.

The materials prepared for the course were designed to enable learners to:

- recognise and value past and present achievements
- assess strengths and weaknesses
- produce an individual development plan
- put into operation one aspect of the plan through a work-based project
- reflect on their experience and performance
- build a personal portfolio to record learning achievements

These 'learning outcomes' were being put in place before the concept of learning outcomes became fashionable. They would not be out of place in any e-portfolio development initiative today, although when this OU project was initiated, the portfolio was paper based (Juwah *et al.,* 2001). The development sowed the seeds of e-portfolio personal development planning at the OU. More significantly it shows how the need for e-portfolios was already established before the systems to support them were in use.

Further examples of paper-based portfolios intended to support students in understanding and reflecting on their learning and skills development followed. One example from the University of Edinburgh is the Personal and Career Development Record. In this example of PDP and portfolio development, a common core of materials and worksheets relevant to disciplines within the Faculty of Arts was prepared to support students in taking control of their personal, academic and career development. In partnership with academic departments, the Career Service developed a series of skills development courses which covered a broad range of employment-related skills such as: teamwork, negotiation, leadership, time management – all of which were linked to academic study to highlight the relevance of these skills both for academic and career success.

The emphasis of the University of Edinburgh project was on supporting the students in recording their achievements and enabling them to understand the processes of reflecting on their learning development. What was clear from this experience was that engaging the students in portfolio development does involve initially high levels of staff input (Ali, 2001). For example, a major role for staff is in helping the students to understand that the portfolio is a tool to support them in reflecting on, and taking control of, their own learning. Learners need to recognise the use of the portfolio for:

- the development of learning process skills
- the development of professional/career related skills
- understanding the concept of reflection on learning
- feedback.

A shift to encouraging development and maintenance of a portfolio does require some realignment of teaching and learning strategies. It is likely that you will need to re-examine your processes for:

- formative assessment
- summative assessment
- acknowledgement and reward for the processes involved in the learning aspects of portfolio development and maintenance.

These are significant changes to the way in which students work, and also the way in which students are supported.

The role of the e-portfolio in assessment will be explored further in Chapters 4 and 5. Those chapters look at the design of courses utilising e-portfolios and the design of assessment of student learning. For now, acknowledging the potential impact of e-portfolios on processes high-lights the connection of portfolio development to other elements within the institution's learning strategies.

The linkage between the concept of the portfolio as a tool to support reflection, and the idea of personal development planning and preparing students for lifelong learning is important in the evaluation of the portfo-lio as a tool for learning. An important step forward is to see the portfolio embedded into learning within a subject area or discipline. The following section provides examples of this.

Embedding the e-portfolio into the curriculum

Depending on your role and responsibilities within a college or univer-sity you are likely to have differing views of the value of an e-portfolio. It is unlikely that senior management staff, lecturers, teachers and tutors would agree even about how to approach the implementation of e-port-folios. Is it feasible to expect all students to develop and maintain an e-portfolio? Would it be better to start off with a pilot project in one sub-ject area with staff who are already enthusiastic about embedding technology into their teaching? While managers may be taking a strate-gic view of what e-portfolios can offer the institution, teachers and tutors will be more concerned about how to use the e-portfolio as a learning tool within specific courses and programmes.

At the University of Strathclyde in Glasgow, Scotland, senior man-agers embraced the idea of embedding personal development planning into the curriculum. Through professional development workshops and seminars, academic staff were encouraged and supported to link per-sonal development planning with the student learning curriculum. There was also a very active programme to enable staff to use new technologies in teaching and learning.

This University prides itself on the level of student support it provides and has always had a very strong record regarding graduate employment. The University Careers Service has a long standing positive reputation for working in partnership with departments to support students in preparing for employment opportunities. The culture of the institution is therefore conducive to staff being innovative in their teaching. One department which had been at the forefront in embedding PDP and e-portfolio development into the curriculum was the School of Pharmacy at the University of Strathclyde. The following case study offers insights into how staff there approached the project.

Case example: Linking the e-portfolio and PDP into a Masters in Pharmacy degree

Staff within the School first agreed some basic principles relating to the e-portfolio:

- Students couldn't be expected to maintain an e-portfolio as an add-on to their other coursework
- The PDP aspect of their learning couldn't be generic, it had to be explicitly embedded within the discipline
- The reflective learning and the e-portfolio needed to be an assessable component of the course
- Assessment relating to PDP and the development and maintenance of the e-portfolio had to be thought through so that students were assessed both on the learning processes and the learning products
- On-going tutor support and formative assessment were important both for the very bright students and for the weaker students who might struggle with the new learning format
- Summative assessment relating to the development and maintenance of the e-portfolio would be an incentive for the students.

The stated aims of the e-portfolio and PDP within the Pharmacy curriculum were:

> *To encourage students to reflect upon and improve the range and level of attainment of their key skills, to develop students' confidence and self-awareness so that they will have an improved ability to learn and make career choices.*

As part of the overall course assessment, it was made clear to the students that there is an expectation that they would:

- Reflect upon and plan their personal development during their study within the Masters in Pharmacy degree programme
- Identify and work towards targets for personal, academic and career development
- Take responsibility for their own learning (including lifelong learning)

- Identify evidence to exemplify their key skills and produce an electronic portfolio of this evidence
- Prepare a CV and/or an application for a pre-registration job in pharmacy.

These points made it clear that the e-portfolio is an integral aspect of the course of study. The overall goal was to enhance employment prospects. The e-portfolio was clearly identified as a tool to support students in the collection and selection of materials to evidence their learning. Students are made aware that they would be working towards standards and performance indicators or learning goals. They were given a clear indication of the key skills they would develop in the course of their studies.

Essop (2004) has demonstrated that students can fail to recognise that they have in fact developed the appropriate key skills in the course of their disciplinary based learning. Students do not always fully appreciate everything that is encompassed within a key skill. With this in mind the School of Pharmacy staff produced a breakdown of what constitutes each key skill. A map showed students where within the curriculum they would develop particular skill sets.

To support the students in understanding the concept of reflection, a self-assessment guide was used. Students were expected to demonstrate their engagement in self-assessment. A 'student skills self-assessment scale', allowed students to easily note their level of attainment against key skills. In this way students diagnosed their own strengths and weaknesses, rating themselves from 1– 4 as follows:

1   I do this very well. I am consistent and successful in it.
2   I am good at this. With some practice I can make it perfect.
3   I am getting better, but still need to work on this a bit more.
4   I am not particularly good at this – yet.

In each year of study the students used this self-assessment scale to:

- identify two or three priority areas for development
- produce an action plan for learning
- discuss this plan with their academic counsellor.

The last point highlights that students were not on their own with this, but expected to engage in dialogue with a tutor/counsellor for the purposes of formative assessment and feedback.

Finally, to discourage an ad hoc approach to portfolio development with no real structure to it, students were encouraged to build their evidence of learning and development by means of a 'diary entry'. Diary entries were expected to:

- identify the skills that the student felt required further development
- state how they identified that skill. In what way did the lack of this skill impede their progress?
- provide a development plan indicating the strategies they would use to evidence development
- give a review or provide evidence of the student's improvement.

In terms of the infrastructure, the e-portfolio in this case was implemented via SPIDER, an ELE constructed within the department (http://spider.pharmacy.strath.ac.uk). The use of SPIDER is described in Chapter 8, where we look at e-portfolio software in more depth. (We include there instructional material provided for students to support them in developing their portfolio (Kane, 2005).)

The students were assigned their personal storage (e-portfolio) area. Here they could collect and organise evidence of their learning, work on their CV or personal profile and store and edit any other artefacts such as assignments, video images, etc. The final output was presented to the students on completion of their studies as a CD-ROM.

In the Strathclyde School of Pharmacy example students were encouraged to use easily accessible resources for further support, and also given extensive induction into the concept of the e-portfolio and into the issues of reflection, self-assessment and self-evaluation. The department enlisted the services of the university educational development unit to support these aspects of students' learning. Because this was an e-portfolio, students could easily develop a list of favourite sites or create links within their e-portfolio to resources they had used or might wish to use.

We have already noted that, if students are expected to develop and maintain an e-portfolio for the purposes of enhancing their learning, it is very important that they see at least one clear benefit to them. In the above example, the e-portfolio was a focal point. The students discussed the contents of their portfolios, and their evidence of learning, with a tutor, departmentally-based advisor or counsellor. Students were expected, as part of the learning process, to self-assess and supported in doing so. They gained credit for maintenance or completion of the portfolio.

This case study highlights a number of important points related to embedding e-portfolios within a course of study:

- The purpose of the e-portfolio must be made clear to the students
- Students require support in the production of a portfolio
- The e-portfolio is a tool to support learning, so it is helpful to provide a clear structure for students to follow.

While the last point might suggest some relinquishing of control of the portfolio by the student, it is not easy to promote self-assessment and reflection. Some guidance and structuring is required. Students will initially be on a steep learning curve and need to understand the direct value of acquiring appropriate skills in developing and using the e-portfolio. We should expect students to go through different developmental stages in acquiring necessary skills. In the Strathclyde case the implementation approach established a very clear link between learning within a disciplinary base, reflecting on learning, personal development planning and lifelong learning.

A more established, extensive example of embedding an e-portfolio into the curriculum comes from Alverno College in Milwaukee. In this case e-portfolios were established at an institutional level rather than at the level of a single department or discipline.

Case example: Alverno – the e-portfolio at an institutional level

Alverno is a Liberal Arts College for women. On its website, it advertises its Diagnostic Digital Portfolio as:

> the first-of-its-kind, web-based system that enables each Alverno student – anyplace, anytime – to follow her learning progress throughout her years of study. It helps the student process the feedback she receives from faculty, external assessors and peers. It also enables her to look for patterns in her academic work so she can take more control of her own development and become a more autonomous learner.
> (Alverno College: http://www.alverno.edu/academics/dpp.html)

Targeted at prospective students, there can surely be no more explicit a statement about the goal and purpose of an e-portfolio. The Diagnostic Digital Portfolio is built upon 'Alverno's student assessment as learning process'. This makes it more transparent to the student. It also provides a useful model to others who seek to understand the educational programme provided at Alverno.

The key points about this use of an Alverno e-portfolio have been identified as:

- a design which assists students to reflect on their academic progress at key points ('integrating moments') in the curriculum and plan for future development
- building on the college's ability-based curriculum framework to provide students with a common language to chart their own progress
- providing a means for students to record their internships, volunteer and community service work and to build an electronic resume
- enabling students and faculty to view it anytime, anywhere they have access to the internet
- a store of multimedia – text, audio and video files
- being fully relational and searchable.

Figure 2.1 shows how the e-portfolio looks to users.

The college has devised a model of the stages students generally move through in the development of their self-assessment skills and reflective learning. This is shown in Table 2.1.

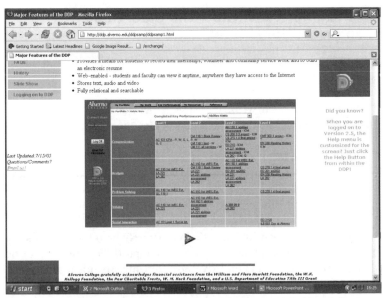

Figure 2.1 Student view of Alverno College Diagnostic Digital Portfolio

Source: http://ddp.alverno.edu/ddpsamp/ddpsamp1.html

Table 2.1 A model for self-assessment/reflective learning: a generic mapping of skills development

Beginning	Student identifies patterns of strengths and weaknesses in behaviour
Intermediate	Student explains the significance of patterns of strengths and weaknesses
Advanced	Student explains components of performance that make it unique and distinctive as part of student's own style

Working with students to give them a sense of how they might use their portfolio as a tool for reflection, teachers and tutors can contextualise the skills within an academic discipline. In doing so, they help students to appreciate the learning expectation within that discipline. The self-assessment/reflective learning map is as much a tool for the staff as for the students. It helps them to relate their practice to the institutional e-portfolio.

A typical skill set to be contextualised within the culture of a discipline might include:

• Communication skills
• Numerical skills
• Reflection
• Critical thinking and analysis
• Historical perspective
• Creativity
• Interpersonal skills (e.g. group work)
• Entrepreneurial skills
• Technological skills
• Commitment and attitude.

This is a 'generic' set of skills. A similar list will be used across many different disciplines. The key is to ensure students actually understand what it means to develop this range of skills within their own discipline. They should also appreciate that as these are generic skills they are also transferable to other contexts.

The very successful Alverno experience suggests that in order to develop an ability to use an e-portfolio purposefully for learning students need:

- an understanding of the skills and comprehension, values and perceptions specific to disciplinary knowledge
- an understanding of the abilities on which they will be assessed both in terms of the products of learning and the process of learning
- debate and dialogue on the legitimacy of a variety of perspectives;
- a good grasp of the nature of evidence for self-assessment
- a shared understanding with their tutors, teachers and lecturers of the necessity and limitations of assessment criteria.

Of course, many of these issues are relevant beyond Alverno. They are appropriate to most teaching and learning contexts in further and higher education. Stating them as explicit prerequisites for e-portfolio success helps us to recognise the opportunity presented through adoption of e-portfolios. For example, at an institutional level it allows us to revisit our conceptions of supporting and facilitating student learning.

What about the technical skills?

How far does the technology, specifically the technical know-how of staff and students, act as a brake on e-portfolio implementation and adoption? So far we have assumed that both staff and students have the necessary ICT skills to cope with development and maintenance of an e-portfolio. We need to bear in mind that this may not necessarily be the case. Even amongst those colleges and universities well advanced in terms of use of e-learning there will be pockets within faculties where there is resistance to use of technology. The reality for e-learning is that there may be departments engaged in excellent practice dispersed throughout any institution. This does not imply an institutional strategy and framework for on-line pedagogies.

Electronic media provide new opportunities for teaching and learning particularly in relation to flexible course delivery. However as Mason (2002) has pointed out, there is a wide spectrum of interest and understanding attached to the term e-learning. In many institutions e-learning has not moved beyond use of the electronic learning environment as a convenient dumping ground for PowerPoint slides and other course resources. Other popular uses are as a convenient way to test students using multiple choice quizzes or as a way of distributing weekly handouts and sending standard messages. It is still quite unusual to find an institution that has undertaken a systematic review of curriculum design, development and delivery to maximise the potential of technology.

This does not mean we should bury our heads in the sand and hope someone else will do the difficult work for us. Most institutions now recognise as inevitable that more emphasis will be put on the use of technology in all aspects of teaching and learning. Teaching material is increasingly prepared and distributed in digital format. As more academic research becomes available online, and sometimes only online, even previously sceptical academics are recognising the value of the internet.

E-portfolios are just one example of the growing use of technology-based teaching and could be utilised as a vehicle for promoting integration of technology in teaching and learning. As they may be used throughout the student's study at the institution, they offer strong motivation for introducing and embedding information literacy skills. These are the skills in handling, manipulating and locating information in digital form, skills that underpin the work of a twenty-first century student. In many universities and colleges the courses which introduce these skills are themselves computer-based or online. An example would be the OU's SAFARI (Skills in Accessing, Finding, and Reviewing Information) (http://www.open.ac.uk/safari). This course is typical in addressing the generic needs of learners who are initially unaccustomed to studying using online tools. The accessing, finding and reviewing skills to which it refers are necessary prerequisites to effective use of e-portfolios. Many of the word-processed documents that students are now required to produce as part of their assessment combine and link to different elements in a manner which could be thought of as similar to mini-portfolios.

Recognising the issues

Confidence in use of technologies within learning, in particular information literacy skills, will be key to the success of an e-portfolio project. It is no coincidence that the interest in e-portfolios coincides with a general re-skilling and up-skilling of college and university staff and students. Interfaces for the e-portfolio which are usable and accessible will obviously also be important. If development and maintenance of an e-portfolio is an integral part of the curriculum we need to be careful that students are not spending too much time learning to use unfamiliar or unfriendly technology. This will discourage use of the e-portfolio for learning opportunities at a time when there are many other alternatives available to students. Picking up on the concerns expressed in the current debate on personalised learning environments (Downes, 2006), if the institution does not provide adequate tools to support students' learning many students will forge and find their own alternatives.

In this chapter we have tried to introduce the reader to some of the current thinking on e-portfolios. We have considered how they, and their immediate 'non-e' precursors, have been used in various educational contexts. There is a strong link between the development of a portfolio and the issue of supporting reflective learning and personal development planning. Development and maintenance of an e-portfolio has to be promoted to the students or learners as a purposeful activity, not something bolted on to their studies as an added extra. Students need to be made aware of the benefits of e-portfolio production for them. Even before this the staff will need to be convinced of the value of an e-portfolio.

As with other areas of e-learning, staff and students need to not only understand the potential of the technology but be equipped with the skills to use it. In both case studies there was an emphasis on the broad range of support that is necessary to integrate e-portfolio use successfully into student learning.

There are clearly many important questions to be worked through within any institution. These centre on considering implementation of e-portfolios as part of student learning and engagement. Some key pointers in initiating an e-portfolio project will be explored in Chapter 3.

Chapter 3

Getting started with e-portfolios

Within any institution, initiating an e-portfolio project or approach to support student learning, represents new challenges. The idea of implementing student learning e-portfolios, in the personal development sense, presents a number of difficulties and opportunities for any institution. Lorenzo and Ittelson (2005) have presented a comprehensive list of issues that we need to think about. These must be addressed to achieve the full potential of e-portfolios in supporting and enhancing student learning. They include:

- Student motivation to maintain an e-portfolio will, to a large extent, be dependent on their understanding of its purpose. How do we ensure that students understand that purpose?
- Will the e-portfolio be an official record of a student's work at subject, programme or institutional level?
- Is e-portfolio development an optional activity or a mandatory activity embedded within the course or programme?
- How long will the e-portfolio remain at an institution after the student graduates? Institutions will need to think about servers, their maintenance and interoperability issues. For example are e-portfolios to be transferable if a student relocates or changes course?
- Who owns the e-portfolio? Does the institution providing the e-portfolio system own certain elements of a student's archived work, similar to other records or transcripts of student's achievement? If the e-portfolio is a document management system for archiving course assignments, who owns and controls the access to such documents?
- Should anyone other than the student be able to make changes to a student's e-portfolio?

- How should an institution promote and support the use of e-portfolios? Who is responsible for promoting an e-portfolio culture within a department or within the institution?
- Who takes responsibility for developing staff skills and understanding so that they are capable and motivated to support students in e-portfolio development?
- How will students' work be assessed in an e-portfolio context? There will be tensions relating to assessment firstly from the point of view of staff conceptions of validity and reliability. There may be concerns over academic integrity in an e-learning environment.
- There could be tensions over the scope of the e-portfolio. If it is too prescriptive students may resent the task. If students are encouraged to be innovative and creative about their learning and about the types of artefacts they show to 'prove' their learning, there might well be issues over how to assess these, and what to assess.

These are just some of the challenging questions and issues that e-portfolio use raises and they will be explored in this chapter. They need to be considered even when the project is a pilot project in one area of study. There are additional challenges when planning to implement e-portfolio use over a whole course or programme. Some of the challenges will be technical, but the biggest impact will be on the way we think about learning and the assessment, or recording, or uses of learning. The most ambitious challenge would be to introduce an institution-wide commitment to using e-learning and e-portfolios.

We need to start by identifying some of the pros and cons that led to the decision whether to adopt e-portfolios. The emphasis that you put on these within your own application of e-portfolios will affect the implementation approach that you take. Once we have answered the 'What to adopt?' and 'What will it mean?' we can then move to consider the 'How?', 'When?' and 'What?' questions.

Considering the pros and cons

The changing nature of the workforce means that for the current population of learners flexibility, adaptability and the importance of how one presents oneself in the job market are key considerations. An important part of learning in higher education is preparing students for life after formal education. This is a new emphasis for many university-level courses. In further education it is often simply a stronger vocational emphasis than previously. The need for portable evidence to demonstrate knowledge and competencies to employers has meant moving beyond the traditional box-file 'repository' of professional practice and career material. Electronic media offer us opportunities to be more sophisticated in how we present ourselves. The e-portfolio affords us a portable and flexible learning, teaching and dissemination tool. It not only meets employer demands but also provides a process, structure and place for learning.

The following points are likely to have informed any institutional discussion around e-portfolio implementation.

The advantages

If implemented well e-portfolios can encourage reflective practice and self-evaluation. The examples of e-portfolios highlighted in Chapter 2 give some insights into how e-portfolios can be designed to fulfil this purpose. They may provide an ongoing basis for students' planning and goal setting. This is dependent upon learners developing skills, knowledge and awareness of the importance of planning and goal setting. They could enable and encourage professional learning and promote self-development. Depending on the target group of students there will be different expectations of the extent and depth of personal development planning and professional development.

They can cater for a wide range of learning styles. Students have different learning strategies and e-portfolios can support this diversity. They enable evidence from a number of different aspects of the curriculum and learning processes to be brought together in one space and can provide a framework for formative and summative assessment. (This will be explored further in Chapters 4 and 5.)

The e-portfolio can help to provide a framework for continuing professional development (CPD) and re-validation or accreditation after graduation. This point shows the potential for the transition from formal learning space into the non-formal learning space beyond the institution. In many careers there are now expectations that an employee will engage in, and show evidence of, regular updating of skills and knowledge through CPD. If the graduate already has the skills of e-portfolio development and maintenance, it should be easier to make the transition to using an e-portfolio for the purpose of CPD.

Alongside the apparent advantages the institution will also have considered the potential disadvantages of e-portfolios. Considering both is important, not only to decide what course of action to take, and what emphasis to place on different features, but also to ensure that expectations among staff are realistic. Depending on your learning context and your students the advantages may weigh more heavily than the disadvantages, or vice versa.

The disadvantages

The disadvantages, or risks, are as numerous as the advantages. Setting up and implementing an e-portfolio project will be a time-consuming process for learners and teachers. As with any new implementation the project has to be well planned. Staff will need to be clear about their roles and responsibilities. Some course and curriculum revision and redesign will probably be necessary which will need to be prepared and resourced, and the support that is needed may not be available.

Care must be taken in clearly defining the purpose and the boundaries of the project. This is not so much a disadvantage as an issue of clarity about the scope of the implementation. The institution needs to be clear about the boundaries of the implementation, just as with any other project. This may mean being realistic and making compromises in terms of what can be achieved in the first stages.

Mentors/facilitators/tutors must be trained or supported in understanding what it means to facilitate student learning in an e-portfolio environment. This preparation is in addition to any purely technical training and can be resource-intensive and expensive. It is unfair on staff to assume they have the skills to manage the processes without preparation. It is also unreasonable to assume that they can make time for additional staff development in already busy schedules. Staff are more likely to be enthusiastic and recognise the relevance of e-portfolios if they are allowed additional time for training and familiarisation. Ideally they should also be consulted about what their development needs might be.

As mentioned previously, learners often don't see the relevance in reflective learning. If staff are introducing e-portfolio use to enhance student learning, one way to improve the appeal of the e-portfolio to student-users will be to ask their opinions. Students may be particularly valuable in identifying the types of technologies that the e-portfolio will need to support. Asking students will also allow you to gain useful and informed insights into how they feel about recording and reflecting on their learning and presenting themselves using different media. You cannot expect students to understand the significance of an e-portfolio without committing time and resources to explaining and negotiating its purpose. Neither can you assume that they will use technology in the same way that you would yourself.

The e-portfolio concept could be viewed as little more than an electronic filing system for a CV and hard evidence of assignments. However it also presents an opportunity to provide a self-directed learning activity for students in which they can identify gaps in their current knowledge skills and competencies. Engaging students in these self-directed learning tasks presents the real challenge for educators. It also presents some of the best opportunities for e-portfolio use.

Implementation issues

As Chapter 2 pointed out, one motivation for introducing e-portfolios is often to support student reflection on learning. This approach to e-portfolio use will have an impact on the ways in which we conceptualise students reflecting on, and recording, their learning and achievement. It will also, if effective, affect the ways in which students themselves reflect on, record, learn and understand their achievements. The focus on re-conceptualising achievement in learning is important. Ideally a reflective e-portfolio implementation will recognise that the e-portfolio is leading us to a change of thinking with regard to the assessment of student learning. This is a complex issue. It implies a big change in behaviour and expectations.

Both will be more achievable if we produce a purposeful plan for the implementation which can be understood by and shared with all the participants in the process. The main issues that your plan will need to include are:

Clear statement of the purpose of the e-portfolio. As we outlined above, there are many different choices to be made in how we choose to use e-portfolios. These will vary according to the learning context. As with any project we need to be clear at the start about what the purpose of our e-portfolio implementation is. Clarifying the purpose – setting clear objectives – will help us to assess whether or not we have been successful. If successful it will help convince others about the value of the implementation.

Determining the scope of the implementation. This follows on naturally from defining the purpose. With any new project you need to consider whether what you plan is achievable and affordable given your resources. If the resources are not available then you may need to modify your plans for the implementation. The issues that we are concerned with here relate to finances, human resources and students. Overly optimistic planning may make participants nervous and erode their confidence in the implementation.

Relating the e-portfolio implementation to the curriculum. You need to be aware of the advantages and disadvantages of the proposed implementation and communicate this to others with regard to the course or curriculum. As with any new initiative in learning and teaching it is helpful to be aware of the pros and cons both from the staff and the student learning perspectives. Your plan should show that you have considered these carefully.

For example, you may be aware of the implications of e-portfolio implementation for your own curriculum area, with your own learners. However, if e-portfolio implementation is to be at institutional, departmental or programme level then you need to know how it will impact on courses beyond your own.

Potential contents for an e-portfolio. What will the e-portfolio be used for across the relevant curriculum areas? You need to answer this question in order to anticipate what the contents may be. Knowing this will help you to identify the technical file types and operational considerations that will underpin the e-portfolio system design. For example will it be able to handle files from specialist Maths software? Will there be file size limitations?

You not only need to show that you have considered what the contents will be but also how they might be viewed, and by whom. For example a 'showcase' e-portfolio will need to be accessible outside the institution and, ideally, beyond the life of the course.

Preparing users to use the e-portfolio. This raises questions of staff and student information and communications technology skills as well as the wider information literacy skills of the participants in the implementation. If staff and students do not already have the requisite skills how will they obtain them? Will these skills be taught as part of the implementation, using the e-portfolio as a training vehicle to contextualise and practice the new skills? Or will the users have a broader requirement for ICT and information literacy skills? Should these be taught as part of the general preparation for study, or wider staff development initiatives?

The e-Learning 'maturity' of the organisation. The extent to which the organisation is already engaging with e-learning, and already uses ICT, is likely to influence the implementation of an e-portfolio system. In some institutions this will be seen as an initiative which is 'in tune' with where the learning and teaching strategy is already leading. In others it may run counter to existing technology initiatives, or simply be too large a step at this stage.

We will now consider each of these implementation and planning issues in more detail.

Clarifying the purpose of the e-portfolio

In Chapter 2 we looked at some of the purposes of an e-portfolio. We know, of course, that one of the purposes may be to replace a paper-based portfolio system. If this is the case then it is reasonable to review what the earlier versions of the portfolio were intended to achieve. Drawing on extensive research from educational settings Snadden *et al.* (1999) suggest that paper-based portfolios:

> contain material collected by the learner over a period of time; that the portfolio is the learner's practical and intellectual property relating to their professional learning and personal development ... that the learner takes responsibility for the creation and maintenance of the portfolio and if appropriate, for presentation of the portfolio for assessment.

Snadden *et al.* note several different purposes here, and these can apply equally to the idea of the electronic portfolio. The portfolio could be viewed as a sort of repository or collection which is owned and operated by the student. It can also serve purposes relating to the student's professional and academic development. The learner should 'take responsibility' but that also implies that the learner has a large degree of control over at least some aspects of the e-portfolio. The portfolio may be used for assessment.

There are currently four common types of conventional portfolio usage in different learning contexts. EPICC, the European Initiatives Co-ordination Committee, provides some useful information on these different types. A brief synopsis is provided below:

Assessment portfolio – this type of portfolio would generally be used in situations where students are not tested or examined in conventional ways, but rather are expected to provide evidence of their competence in particular subject areas. Students may provide photographs, video recordings, reflective reports. They may also be expected to include information such as employer or supervisor evaluations of their competence.

> Portfolios of this nature have particular benefits in assessment of work-based learning. They are also very useful in situations where assessment may not be something that can be done under normal 'test' conditions because the situation is a one-off, or the work is extremely large and immobile. For example art installations where it is important to see the work in situ, or fitting a patient with a

prosthesis, where the assessor needs to view the student's work in the context of the particular patient. In both these cases the student is working with a one-off product and can better explain and show their work through a video clip of their practice, supported by documents (working drawing and patient notes) created over time. The snapshot in time offered by conventional assessment does not work well in either of these cases.

The beauty of this type of e-portfolio is that it can be designed to be easy to use but still allow for flexibility and creativity in the way students present evidence of their work and their achievements. Students can also be saved the pressure of having to produce all their assessed work within a very short time-frame as they will 'build' their portfolio over the life of the course.

(Banks, 2004)

Showcase portfolio – this type of portfolio might be thought of as being closest to our conventional view of portfolios. We are already familiar with the portfolios developed by artists or architects. With this form of portfolio students are free to determine the content but they tend to display their best work. In addition to the work itself they may also display the 'workings' and any reviews or evaluations. A showcase portfolio could be used for presenting oneself to potential employers. A logical structure might be one that emulates a curriculum vitae.

Traditionally such portfolios might be expected to be large physical entities to be carried around. As they contained 'original' work there would likely be only one copy which the student would present in person (not trusting it to the care of someone else). The items in it could be physically damaged and might well be irreplaceable. The e-portfolio overcomes problems of physical bulk as well as the problems of replication and dissemination. In addition it offers the student the potential to show work using multiple media opening up more innovative ways of presenting work. Student project work in many different subject areas, not just art and architecture, would be amenable to presentation in a showcase e-portfolio.

(Banks, 2004)

The development portfolio – this is again one of the ideas described in Chapter 2. It is the sort of use introduced in the case example from the University of Strathclyde, School of Pharmacy. A major role for the development portfolio is to support students' personal development planning (PDP). This type of portfolio is well suited to a situation where students all take the same courses, try to achieve the same goals and are tested or assessed in the same ways. The e-portfolio provides a means of tracking and planning the development of the students over time. It also provides a clear record of what each student has done which could follow the student as they change course or institution, or be referred to by more than one institution at a time.

Reflective portfolios – this sort of e-portfolio has the over-arching purpose of self assessment and evaluation. There is similarity with the other three types of portfolio (assessment, evaluation and development). However the reflective portfolio is more clearly the property of the student and specific to their needs. The expectation would be that the owner presents within their folio written reflections around particular competencies. Through the reflective portfolio the learner might be expected to show accomplishments and how these relate to the learning goals.

> The reflective portfolio is fairly common in teacher education and is often used for courses aimed at lecturers in FE and HE. Students can provide lesson plans, peer observations, student evaluation sheets, etc. as a basis for reflection-on-action, revisiting and reviewing their classroom practice. Another application of the reflective portfolio, this time within medical education, would be to provide student reflections on handling patients. The key ideas behind the reflective portfolio are similar to the idea of paper based 'learning journals'.
>
> (Tartwijk and Driessen, 2004)

Determining the scope of the implementation

There is no shortage of examples of e-portfolio initiatives ranging from individual course pilot projects to national projects. Although we expect readers of this book to be primarily interested in institutional, departmental, programme or course e-portfolios, awareness of larger projects may also be appropriate. Two examples are mentioned briefly here.

In the UK the Royal College of Nursing is typical of a professional organisation exploring and encouraging the use of e-portfolios. It offers its members a portfolio template and framework to support their continuing professional development (CPD). Production of a portfolio, containing reflections on practice and evidence of CPD, is a requirement for accreditation. The portfolio is considered a more valid means of assessment when testing attitudes and professionalism that are difficult to assess by other methods. As nurses are required to undergo periodic re-accreditation this is very significant. In nursing courses there is now a requirement to equip new nurses with the skills to maintain a portfolio. Starting an e-portfolio while a student, then maintaining it through transition to work and across employers, is considered a realistic requirement. In this example, the largest employer of nurses in the UK (the National Health Service) has set out a template and framework for the portfolio. With other professional organisations there may be less clarity, more confusion, about the form the development e-portfolio should take.

On an even broader scale there can be national e-portfolio projects. As part of its strategy to address the issue of the digital divide, the Welsh Assembly has embarked on a major project to offer all of its three million citizens the opportunity to develop an individual e-portfolio (EPICC, 2006). This recognises that an e-portfolio, and the skills needed to develop and maintain one, could in the future be widely beneficial to all citizens. Some ideas around this are explored in Chapter 10 where we consider several future scenarios for e-portfolios.

On an institutional or local level, the scope of the implementation will be influenced by finances, human resources (the person power to complete the task), and students (the end-users and their appreciation of the project).

- *Finances:* You need to determine what the resource investment in the project will be. For a very local pilot you may have the resources for implementation within programme or departmental budget. Even if this is the case, you also need to consider what will happen if the project is a success? Will you need or want to develop it further? What will be the financial implication of success? The persistence of the e-portfolio (its ability to be accessed in the future) is an important aspect of its usefulness.

  Where the funding has to be sought from the institution, or some external funder, you will need to show clear and convincing costings for the implementation. This will involve projections of use and some form of risk analysis. You should be realistic about the costs and the risks – for example failure to successfully adapt or implement the technology in time and on budget. It may be necessary to restrict the use of the e-portfolio system in early years, or limit the scope of the system, so that it can be realistically resourced. An over-stretched system with no operational slack may result in a failure of your project simply because it runs out of money.

- *Human resources:* Which staff need to be involved in developing and introducing e-portfolios? Are they available? Although you may so far have championed e-portfolios yourself, this level of support will not stretch across a large project in a sustainable way. Your implementation team will probably include technical staff and e-portfolio experts, but should also identify those teaching and support staff who will be used to implement e-portfolios across different aspects of the curriculum. You will need to know whether these staff are available to work with you, and also whether they have some motivation to do so. Are they interested? If not you will need to consider how could you make them interested.

Depending on the prior experience of staff you are involving, you may need to factor in a training and familiarisation period. You will certainly need to address the question of whether it will be possible to attract and recruit specialist staff or train existing colleagues.

- *Students:* Although it is possible to implement an e-portfolio without initial student involvement, they are obvious sources of information and ideas at the implementation stage and during any pilot. For example usability testing with students will help to identify accessibility and other technical interface problems before they cause difficulties for the course. More significantly, students will help you to understand what will make an e-portfolio work for them. They are also the obvious source of information on how best to motivate students to use the e-portfolio when it is finished. At the least you will need to make sure that any student participants understand from the beginning what the e-portfolio project might mean for their learning. Whether it achieves any transformative potential will be largely determined by the level and type of student participation.

Relating the e-portfolio implementation to the curriculum

Setting up an e-portfolio project and embedding the concept into the curriculum is one aspect of encouraging students to use the tool for learning. But introducing e-learning and e-portfolios into the learning context is the beginning of a shift in the teaching and learning paradigm. The extent that shift progresses will depend on the goals of the institution and the scope of the project. Most of the current literature presents the e-portfolio as an element of the wider processes of teaching and learning. The overarching issue is the pedagogical principles underpinning the rationale for implementing e-portfolios into the curriculum.

The following diagram illustrates the way in which an e-portfolio initiative can be situated within a wider teaching and learning process.

There are clearly tensions inherent within implementation about encouraging students to develop and maintain an e-portfolio. If the e-portfolio is intended to support students in reflection there are issues relating to ownership that need to be considered. For example, should students be expected to present their reflections for scrutiny for the purpose of 'high stakes assessment'?

Barrett asserts that there are two contradictory e-portfolio purposes: formative and summative evaluation (or assessment). She believes that 'unless these conflicting paradigms and competing purposes underlying portfolios are recognised, their value for learning may be subverted. Electronic portfolio technologies promise support for both high stakes assessment and deep student learning' (Barrett and Carney, 2005).

Barrett however believes these dual purposes are frequently in conflict and that we have not yet fully come to terms with the educational and pedagogic issues associated with e-portfolios.

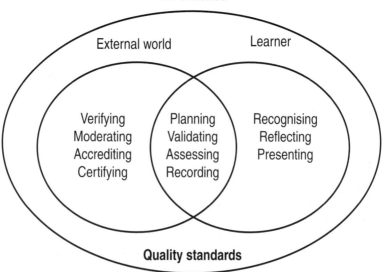

Figure 3.1 Processes and ownership in developing e-portfolios

Source: G. Attwell, 2005, Recognising Learning: Educational and pedagogic issues in e-Portfolios, http://elgg.net/gattwell/weblog/2613.html

When embarking on an e-portfolio project it is important to be aware that there are tensions relating to pedagogical purpose and that it is worthwhile delving more deeply into the research literature as the project progresses. It is clear that there are wider considerations relating to e-learning and how it is changing our conceptions of ownership, construction of knowledge and assessment of student learning. (Assessment of student learning in an e-portfolio context is a subject we return to in Chapter 5.)

The current trend towards knowledge construction as a learning paradigm requires that students be encouraged and supported explicitly in developing information literacy skills. To achieve this in courses and programmes of study gives good reason for encouraging maintenance of a portfolio in which students record their personal learning experiences, and make explicit their learning processes.

In practice e-portfolios can be used in a wide range of learning contexts and may combine characteristics of the showcase, development and reflective portfolios described above. In general terms the point of the portfolio is to encourage students to underpin their learning with various kinds of evidence, often collected over the duration of the course. This can include worksheets, products, evaluations, video clips or other artefacts. The variety of the content will in part depend on the discipline and the teaching approaches as well as the individual student. At stages along the way, a subset of the e-portfolio, or the entire thing, can be used to validate and facilitate assessment of student learning. As with other aspects of teaching, the linking of e-portfolio use with assessment is generally a major driving force to ensure both staff and students take the portfolio seriously.

Whatever your chosen goals or purposes for the e-portfolio, whatever your discipline area, it will be useful to seek out examples of models of e-portfolio projects. Until we have a greater range of projects to draw from these may not necessarily match your own learning environment or context, and they may be portfolio rather than e-portfolio projects.

The example of personal development planning in the School of Pharmacy at the University of Strathclyde, Glasgow was described earlier. This is an example of an implementation into the curriculum which offers as incentives for students both formative feedback on their learning and assessment credit for 'completion' of the e-portfolio – in other words the e-portfolio is a component of summative assessment.

The significance of the e-portfolio was thus emphasised to students: students were told that they could not graduate without having completed the portfolio. They were encouraged to use it for PDP, but were expected to produce a finished e-portfolio for assessment. Because the primary purpose was PDP the e-portfolio was not graded. To allocate marks for a PDP (rather than simply check that it is there and complete) might well intimidate students into being guarded about their development needs, defeating some of the purpose of the PDP. This unbundling of 'performance measurement' and 'developmental review' is one that you are probably familiar with within your own careers. Best practice in human resource management suggests that conflating of performance reviews and professional development discussions results in conflicts for both participants. Where the e-portfolio is intended to be reflective there may even be an argument for the teacher or tutor not seeing it at all, or only having access to elements which the student chooses to share.

The Diagnostic Digital Portfolio (DDP) from Alverno College, Milwaukee gives us an example where the teaching and learning context is built upon the e-portfolio concept. Here the e-portfolio is a fundamental aspect of the curriculum. It is intended to support student learning; there is a strong emphasis on reflection and encouragement of students to take responsibility for their learning. Students choosing to pursue their studies at Alverno College know from the start that the DDP is an integral aspect of the teaching and learning contract. The DDP is also an element of the course over which students have a large degree of control, encouraging their development as autonomous learners.

As can be seen from the above examples, the scope of e-portfolio projects can vary enormously. As with any new educational initiative or innovation, e-portfolio implementation needs to be planned carefully to suit the context. Technology should not be used for the sake of it. It should only be introduced if it is clear that technology-mediated teaching and learning will enhance the student experience.

The following checklist is intended as a guide to the questions you should be asking to determine what the impact on your teaching and support may be. Not all of these questions are relevant to every teaching and learning situation, but they should give you some idea of the issues to weigh up when considering the implementation of e-portfolios.

1 What is your target group? What you can expect of your students will depend on the type of learning institution, the stage of learning and the subject area(s).
2 Are your students ready for e-portfolio-based learning? Is it appropriate for your target group?
3 Is it clear that all of the students in the target group(s) have the appropriate IT literacy skills to manage and maintain an e-portfolio?

It is easy to assume that in our so-called 'technological world' all learners have access to computers or have used computers for a variety of purposes, but this is not necessarily the case.

4   How will you introduce the portfolio to the learners? You may want your students to develop an e-portfolio to support their IT literacy skills or as a repository for assignments.

5   Will you have a standardised format for the e-portfolio? Deciding on whether or not to have a standardised format will have implications for setting up templates or deciding how much creative freedom students will have in the development of their portfolio.

6   Will the e-portfolio be a public or a private document? You may want to encourage your students to have private areas in their e-portfolio and areas that they share with teachers, tutors, peers. These considerations have implications for the structure of the portfolio.

7   How will the learners be supported during the e-portfolio development process? You may need to decide whether the development of the e-portfolio is in itself a learning task to be assessed or whether an e-portfolio 'space' will be set up for all students and it is the portfolio content that will be assessed.

8   Who will undertake to review the portfolio with the learners? It is important that the e-portfolio is not a dislocated task for the students. In many situations it is likely that students will need formative feedback on the development and upkeep of their e-portfolios.

9   What training and support will be available to help the assessors/reviewers work with students on their e-portfolios? Some staff may be well ahead in their thinking about embedding technology into their teaching, others may be skilful in using ICT for some purposes but don't have experience of working with e-portfolios – or designing courses around e-portfolios.

10   What will happen to students who don't want to keep an e-portfolio? If e-learning or e-portfolios are a part of the course or programme this information should have been publicised in course or curriculum information. If it is a core and compulsory part of the course then students may fail the course because they cannot, or will not keep an e-portfolio. Are you comfortable with that? If e-portfolio use is made optional what will be the implications for curriculum design?

This list of questions is by no means exhaustive. Considering these questions, and others relevant to the e-portfolio project, could provide a useful basis for a staff development exercise around implementation of such a project.

Potential contents for an e-portfolio

So far the emphasis has been on the e-portfolio as a tool to support reflection on learning. However we do also need to consider the content. What could be included in the e-portfolio to provide the basis for reflection? Table 3.1 provides an indication of the types of information that may be stored in the e-portfolio. It is not an exhaustive list, but it has been compiled from examples and commentaries on e-portfolios drawn from a wide range of sources. Taken together with the agreed purpose of the e-portfolio, it will provide guidance on setting up an e-portfolio framework for your own learning context.

As more information becomes available on e-portfolios, common themes are emerging. Colleges and universities in the USA are well advanced in e-portfolio implementations. Their views of the e-portfolio are changing the culture of learning. For example, there is a growing emphasis on the idea of 'authentic assessment', often defined as 'assessment related to the "normal" application of the knowledge, skills and understanding being assessed – or "real world" applications'

Table 3.1 Type of e-portfolio content

Content	Explanation
Coursework	This could range from short assignments, information relating to assignments, to extensive projects. The formats could include text, video, audio and multimedia.
Assessments	Could include formative feedback through to summative assessments.
Pieces of work relating to life-long learning	This may include CVs, job applications, course presentations, 'artefacts' of students' choice.
Reflections on achievements, goals, outcomes	For example, students' self-assessments of skills development, ideas on improving on current attainment.
Transcripts, records of achievement	This may mean for the students a mapping of course results and courses completed
Evidence of competencies, learning outcomes achieved	Could relate to work-based learning, and supervisors' reports.
Planning and reflection	Relating to personal development planning, space for a learning journal or diary.
Self and peer feedback information	May relate to project work, peer and group learning, shared space in the portfolio.

(Elton, 2003). The changing nature of the student population is blurring the boundaries between learning through work placement and 'formal' college or university learning. These changes all begin to make sense of the idea of the e-portfolio as a tool to encourage learner autonomy and individual responsibility for learning – although we may still be some way from achieving this goal.

Preparing users to use the e-portfolio

Implementing e-learning and e-portfolios into a course or curriculum is obviously dependent upon staff and students having the necessary technical skills and knowledge as well as an appreciation of what the e-portfolio is for. There must be some motivation for busy students and staff to acquire additional skills. If these are recognised as transferable or 'generic' skills, with wide applicability, participants may be more willing to learn them. For example the nursing student who knows that her future career success will depend in part on competence in e-portfolio administration will be well motivated to learn more about using and maintaining them. Instruction in creating and editing different file types will be seen, by many students, as broadly relevant to a range of study and non-study activities. Arguably it is the technical and not the learning uses of the e-portfolio that are likely to be regarded as 'new work' by staff. But if users – particularly the staff teaching with this system – lack an appropriate level of technical skill and are unfamiliar with, or confused by, the e-portfolio software, the initiative is unlikely to be a success.

Acquiring the relevant level of skills may require staff and students to update and upgrade their skills through appropriate hands-on staff development programmes. The precise skills required will depend on the purpose, the scope and the framework for e-portfolios that you have chosen. If users have not engaged in using computers for learning previously they need to understand that developing ICT skills is an ongoing process. The skills that they require to remain competent will probably change over time. This is particularly important in preparing for e-portfolio use. The e-portfolio user is expected to be able to produce their own work rather than relying too heavily on the technical skills of others. Unless a baseline of technical skill is developed there will be a question about whose work is being commented on or assessed. There will generally be other opportunities for using these skills in preparing other non-portfolio work during their studies. Skills such as webpage design, video and audio editing may even have applicability for their leisure interests.

Here are some suggested approaches to upgrading staff and student with basic technical skills:

1   Computer fundamentals – a course covering an introduction to computing; instruction on the use of common applications such as word processing, spreadsheet and database programs; using computers for problem solving.
2   Presentation applications – instruction on using desktop publishing software; PowerPoint; graphics applications.
3   Multimedia technologies – learning to create a presentation combining text, graphics, audio and video links. Learning how to navigate, interact, create and communicate information and ideas using graphics presentation programs.
4   Database application development – learning how to manage information using a database. Designing a database structure to sort, analyse and display data effectively.
5   Computer graphics and animation – learning to use graphic design software to create, manipulate and enhance graphic images suitable for various publication formats. Creating your own digital videos.

This list suggests some approaches that students and staff should recognise as relevant to creating interesting and useful content within the e-portfolio. Selection of user-friendly and accessible applications with built-in help systems will also obviously be helpful. Easy-to-use systems and timely relevant training opportunities will prevent many users from spending more time and energy grappling with the technology than learning from use of the e-portfolio.

In parallel with the support that students need in learning how to use basic technologies and specific software, students should also be given opportunities to acquire and practice their information literacy skills. Oblinger and Hawkins advise that 'information literacy skills include cognitive activities such as acquiring, interpreting and evaluation of the quality of information' (2006: 13). Where the course draws on electronic resources and content, or requires students to generate it, the emphasis of these skills may be on using the internet effectively as a parallel resource with campus based services such as the library.

Although students are not usually explicitly assessed on these skills they are increasingly implicit within the curriculum. Some years ago Breivik (1998) described information literacy skills as the most important skill set with which our graduating students should be equipped. She asserted that academic institutions will have failed their students if they do not enable them to become autonomous, independent lifelong learners who can access, evaluate and effectively use information. Educational institutions must assume some responsibility for creating independent learners who will be able to learn not only within the confines of the institution but in their workplace, their social environment and throughout their lives. While most students today are well able to access information electronically, we should be concerned that they understand the importance of having good information literacy skills. As educators we know that the information available online is not always reliable or high quality. In fact it sometimes offers a very good proving ground for undergraduates who need to demonstrate that they know how to acquire, interpret and evaluate information in an academic context. In an age where information is so easily accessed through the internet, students need to develop critical analytical skills to be able to assess issues of quality and bias in the information they locate.

The variety of sources from which the student e-portfolio builder may be acquiring information offers specific challenges. Not least is the knowledge that the showcase e-portfolio type (and perhaps also elements of developmental and reflective e-portfolios) will be open to inspection by others beyond the institution. This adds additional pressures to ensure that students and staff using e-portfolios understand the legal, ethical and intellectual property and copyright issues in reusing or versioning information.

The e-learning 'maturity' of the organisation

The communicative potential of e-learning is giving rise to a generation of courses and programmes of study which employ a social constructivist approach to learning (MacDonald, 2004). This means using on-line media to support distributed collaborative interaction and dialogue, access to information and resources and a greater push towards understanding rather than knowing. It also involves encouraging students to engage in technology-mediated social interaction and collaboration.

This is a challenge in both e-learning and 'traditional' classroom teaching and learning environments. Do our students understand the concept of collaborative learning? Are they attuned to the ideas of information exchange and knowledge construction? Would they be able to participate in on-line conferencing and internet searching with fellow students?

The challenges are not only to students and their readiness. Are we clear ourselves about the potential of shifting paradigms? Are we comfortable with giving students more control and ownership of their learning? Do we truly see the value of the e-portfolio to support and promote student learning?

One way of answering these questions is to look at the level of e-learning maturity within your organisation. The work on e-learning maturity is linked to Scott Morton's 'waterfall' model describing three successive stages of IT adoption – evolutionary, through to transitional and ending in revolutionary (Scott Morton, 1991). There were six stages along the way:

1   Individualised
2   Localised
3   Co-ordinated
4   Transformative
5   Embedded
6   Innovative.

Although Scott Morton's work was based in business and not educational organisations it has been used by researchers in the UK to look at

Table 3.2 Student opportunity for autonomy in internal assessment across the institution

Localised	There is no recognised student autonomy
Co-ordinated	Some staff in some of the subject teaching encourage students (at appropriate level for their age) to mark and record their own or peer performances
Transformative	Most staff encourage students when appropriate, to mark and record their own or peer performances. No systematic evaluation of this innovation takes place.
Embedded	There is a clear policy of involving students in the assessment and monitoring of their work. For example: • Students contribute to online portfolios which can be used as an alternative measure of authentic assessment to track student performance • Students mark and record their own and peer performances
Innovative	There is a clear policy of involving students in the assessment and monitoring of their work. The innovation is carefully monitored and good practice is rolled out across the institution.

Source: Underwood and Dillon (2004)

e-learning adoption in educational institutions. For example Underwoood and Dillon (2004) created a comprehensive set of institutional self-assessment matrices for use by schools and colleges, which concentrate on the last five of Scott Morton's stages.

If we look at Underwood and Dillon's definition of the 'Localised' to 'Innovative' stages for their 'Student opportunity for autonomy' criterion, we see that they mention online portfolios (Table 3.2).

This is only one criterion out of 75, but it indicates that in terms of e-maturity modelling, researchers would expect to see e-portfolio use typically in institutions which were making *embedded* or *innovative* use of ICT. If your own institution is not yet at this stage of e-learning development it would be worth considering whether an e-portfolios project could be sustained. Are you ready for e-portfolios?

Summary and online resources

The published literature relating to e-portfolios often does not include the fundamental issues that need to be considered if the implementation of an e-portfolio project within an educational context is to be successful. This chapter has outlined for the reader some of these issues. The purpose and scope of the project needs to be clearly defined and communicated to both students and staff. The skills required by users to undertake the creation, management and marking of an e-portfolio also need to be determined. Attention must be given to the information technology and information literacy skills required of students and if necessary curricula may need to be redesigned to incorporate these skills. Finally the potential of incorporating technology into teaching and learning may require a shift in paradigm shift for the future.

While each e-portfolio implementation will have peculiar and particular implementation issues, the following online resources offer further advice on issues your implementation may need to take account of.

Di Biase, D. (2002) *Using e-Portfolios at Penn State to Enhance Student Learning – Status, Prospects, and Strategies,* online at http://www.e-education.psu.edu/portfolios/e-port_report.shtml>.

Gathercoal, P., Love, D., Bryde, B., McKean, G. (2002) '*On implementing web-based electronic portfolios*', *Educause Quarterly* 25(2): 29–37, online at http://www.educause.edu/ir/library/pdf/eqm0224.pdf>.

The E-Learning Framework (2004) *What is an ePortfolio?* online at <http://www.elframework.org.projects/petal/whatiseportfolio/view?searchter m=e-portfolios>.

Portal of papers entitled *Getting Started,* online at http://www.elearn.malts.ed.ac.uk/eportfolio/start.phtml>

Yancey, K. (2006) An Exercise in Absence, online at http://www.campus-tech-nology.com/news_article.asp?id=17795&typeid=155>.

Chapter 4

Course design using e-portfolios

As has been indicated in earlier chapters, one of the best ways of ensuring that students develop a portfolio is to integrate it into a course. However, e-portfolios to date have been used largely as an institutional device to demonstrate student progress over time (e.g. to external quality assurance inspectors) or to assess learning rather than as part of learning. Recent technological enhancements to e-portfolio software have broadened the available features such that it is now possible to integrate the learning outcomes of a course and the use of e-portfolios. In this section four ways of building a course around e-portfolios are discussed.

There is undoubtedly an unresolved tension in the use of e-portfolios in higher education between institutional control of the process and of the software, and individual student ownership of the content. All of the current evidence points to the need for students to feel that their e-portfolio belongs to them. Furthermore, the underlying pedagogy of e-portfolio use draws on theories of constructivism, student-centred learning and authentic educational activities. Student engagement with the process of building and maintaining their e-portfolio is critical to the success of any application, so appropriate course design should be focused on achieving high levels of engagement.

It is a cliché to say that we are daily bombarded with a plethora of information which we can scarcely process. Nevertheless, in tertiary education we need to provide students with the skills to manage this overload in ways which reflect society's changing relationship with information. E-portfolios offer a facility for doing this if they are fully integrated into the design of courses.

How to engage students with their e-portfolio

One of the main issues with the use of e-portfolios is how to ensure that students are sufficiently motivated to actually engage with them on a regular basis. When online communication first became available as an educational tool, the same problem was evident: how to engage students with the process of interacting online? Successful approaches to each of these situations are not dissimilar. There are three ways of creating an environment in which students will be willing to both build and maintain an e-portfolio:

1   Make it fun and connect its use to the course
2   Integrate the e-portfolio software with their online workspace
3   Give students ownership of the process and control of the product.

Students use mobile phones and many other technologies in their leisure time. If students are given the tools to control the look and feel of their portfolios, to create dynamic, innovative presentations of their work and experiences, they are more likely to engage with the process beyond the formal course requirements. Motivation is one of the most significant elements of engagement and hence of learning. For those students who are skilled in design or who want to develop such skills, there should be the resources and the flexibility to create visually expressive e-portfolios. However, for those who do not have these skills and are not interested in developing them, templates should be provided to help them easily create professional-looking e-portfolios.

A note of caution needs to be sounded in terms of both quality and learning outcomes. If e-portfolios become a jumbled collection of photos, artefacts, unconnected ramblings and other media-rich items, they may have been 'fun' to assemble, but they have lost their educational value. The aim in making e-portfolios fun and student-centred has to be balanced by the equally important aim of making them a learning experience. This can be accomplished by setting a standard for e-portfolio work, for example by providing guidelines which clearly reinforce the learning objectives, by making available examples of e-portfolios which demonstrate the desired content and quality, and by reinforcing the adage that with ownership comes responsibility. Giving ownership of any learning process to the learner does not mean that the teacher abrogates all responsibility. In fact, quite the opposite is the case. Providing scaffolding, resources, structure and advice are in many ways a more demanding role for the teacher than telling students what to do and to think.

The most important way to make the e-portfolio an integral part of a learner's daily routine is to ensure that the software is integrated into the tasks students regularly perform for their courses in the electronic learning environments (ELEs). In this case, tight integration between the e-portfolio system and the ELE makes portfolio building another simple step in a student's daily learning routine. These integration points should be seamless and transparent, allowing students to move easily from their course to their portfolio.

Course design parameters

Ehrmann provides a salutary comment about e-portfolios by noting that:

> Using an electronic portfolio does not, by itself, create any magical kind of improvement in education. The software may cost money and using it consumes valuable time. However, if faculty and students can use the portfolio to alter teaching/learning activities – that's where the potential payoffs can be found.
>
> (Ehrmann, 2004)

In this section we discuss four ways of using e-portfolios in course design to create engaging activities. First and foremost of these is the process for which e-portfolios are most appreciated: encouraging reflective learning. The second is the skill of setting goals and understanding how to achieve them. Related to goal setting is the third area of peer commenting and self-assessment. Finally and most notable is the fourth aspect of course design: communication skills. The essential factor in all four of these uses of an e-portfolio is that they must be directly related to the learning outcomes of the course. Students have a strong radar system for detecting any aspect of a course which is not really critical to their final mark.

Before beginning to design a course which uses an e-portfolio, it is important to consider what changes or improvements are anticipated by introducing this technology. Is the e-portfolio intended to support students in a primarily online course? What other technologies are students expected to use on the course and will they all be new or will some be familiar already? Is the e-portfolio a supplement to face-to-face teaching and if so, what existing activities does it replace? In short, what are the outcomes which an e-portfolio is intended to underpin? If teachers are unsure of this or have introduced e-portfolios because they are the trendy new technology, there will be resistance from students. It is very easy to provide e-portfolio software, but it takes real course design know-how to achieve successful student engagement with the process.

Reflective learning

The practice of reflection has become a prominent tool for learning in recent years. One definition of it is the following:

> Reflection is a form of mental processing that we use to fulfil a purpose or to achieve some anticipated outcome. It is applied to gain a better understanding of relatively complicated or unstructured ideas and is largely based on the reprocessing of knowledge, understanding and possibly emotions that we already possess.
>
> (Moon, 2005)

Successful uses of e-portfolios in higher education inevitably ascribe a key role to reflection in the design of the course. As the definition suggests, structuring the practice of reflection transforms it into a learning experience. For example, the teacher may provide prompts to help students connect their reading with the core issues of the course. The affective dimension of reflection is also an important part of the process and one with which students may well need guidance. They may need encouragement to use the 'first person' in their reflective writing and to acknowledge the significance of feelings in the learning process.

One very effective way of structuring reflective activities is to relate them to the learning objectives of the course. Documents, project plans and an annotated bibliography might also be organised around the objectives along with the reflective pieces of work. Frequent feedback may be required to prompt students to think further about issues, and to consider other perspectives.

Reflection is not something to be carried out only at the end of an activity or learning experience. Reflection should be a continuous process throughout the study period. At the beginning of a course it is useful for students to reflect on what they don't know, what they would like to learn and how they want to go about it. Students might then work in small groups to identify useful resources to address their knowledge gaps. They might also form larger discussion groups to evaluate the resources they have found. Students might be required to keep a learning journal throughout the course in which they record their thoughts, observations, feelings and questions. It is up to the teacher or tutor to direct students' attention to other resources or to further questions. This process is facilitated by the e-portfolio software which allows the student to share parts or all of the growing portfolio with named people.

Many students will need help in understanding what reflection means in an academic context. For this reason it is useful to provide examples of reflective writing and to build an activity around them by asking students to evaluate what learning is being gained through the reflective process. One of the barriers to learning through reflection is that students rely on formulaic responses to reflection exercises. This may be prevented by studying examples of authentic reflection and by the teacher referring to the examples if students appear to be floundering.

Reflection is an essential feature of a deep approach to learning. It is inappropriate and unnecessary on a course whose aim is to impart a large corpus of information for students to digest and reiterate on the exam at the end.

Reflection seems to be a part of the kinds of learning in which learners try to understand material that they encounter and to relate it to what they already knew. Relating new material to what one knows already may mean reflecting on what one knows and modifying it (deep approach). Reflection does not seem to have a role in the learning in which learners try just to retain new information without creating deep links with the new ideas (surface approach). Reflection will also be involved in the process of representing learning – when, for example, a learner's understanding is tested in a format that demands reprocessing of the ideas (e.g. an essay). It is less or uninvolved in an approach that requires reiteration of the responses in the same format as the original knowledge (Moon, 2005).

An example of an activity that helps students to relate new material to what they already know is called a 'critical incident diary,' which works very well in e-portfolio software. This involves students describing instances of learning over a period of about a week. Examples might include solving a problem, encountering a new idea, resolving a conflict or enjoying a novel experience. The purpose in writing about these instances is first of all to observe them, second to be able to describe them and finally to consider what was learnt from them. If the learning can be related to course issues, so much the better.

Should reflection be assessed? This is a question which divides practitioners down the middle. Some say that it is not appropriate to 'grade peoples' feelings'. Others contend that it will only be valued by students if it does contribute to their final mark. What is obvious is that the teacher needs to think carefully about how to assess the reflective component of the course. Three factors are critical:

- The reflective activities need to be directly related to the learning outcomes of the course.
- The reflective activities need to be appropriate to the level and content of the course.
- Students need to receive adequate preparation and feedback from the teacher about the reflection process.

If these guidelines are followed, assessing the reflective element of an e-portfolio can contribute to students' intrinsic motivations for learning.

Herrington and Oliver (2002) describe the method they used to encourage reflection on a graduate level online course. This involved a learning journal and a continuous process of reflecting on their work. However, the central feature of the process was their use of an authentic task, chosen by the student, as the focus of the work: 'It is entirely up to the student to propose a task that suits their own particular circumstances, with the proviso that their work is informed by current literature, and that they consciously reflect on the process as it is happening' (2002: 317).

The other significant aspect of the process was that students had access to a variety of online resources and supports: a list of books and relevant texts, links to online journal articles on reflection and a website which helped students structure their reflection on the task. The authors note that a complex task requiring decision-making and reasoning is required in order that students appreciate the need for reflection.

At undergraduate level, a number of practitioners recommend dual entry procedures to support students in understanding the nature and value of reflection (see Hatton and Smith, 1995). So, for example, in the first column students might describe a learning experience or summarise an issue from the course material. In the second column, they write a critical reflection on the experience or issue. In this way students learn to distinguish between description and reflection, and are empowered to consider their own thoughts and feelings about their learning.

The aim of developing reflective learners is to encourage students to be more self-aware and self-critical; to be honest about themselves, and open to criticism and feedback. An e-portfolio with structured reflective processes and mentoring by the teacher can instil these qualities in students. Activities which require students to be objective in weighing up evidence or which encourage them to be open to, and prepared to try different approaches fit well within an e-portfolio framework. Ultimately this method of teaching helps to develop independent lifelong learners.

Goal setting

Teaching students the skill of setting goals for themselves is, like reflection, a life skill which should be one of the outcomes of a higher education degree. Goal setting can be implemented across a whole undergraduate or graduate career, but it can usefully be practised on a smaller scale within a specific course. In this section we discuss the use of an e-portfolio for both kinds of goal setting. As with reflection, goal setting is a skill with which many students will have had little or no prior experience. Thus it will require support, resources and feedback provided by a teacher or mentor.

While the use of an e-portfolio over a whole programme is becoming relatively common especially at American universities and colleges, it is rather rare to find goal setting by the student on individual courses. This is a pity, as it fits well with a student-centred approach to learning and with the use of e-portfolios as a technology to support the approach.

The early adopters of e-portfolios have discovered that students have difficulty grasping the notion of lifelong learning skills such as goal setting and reflective learning. Finding effective ways of giving students the experience and environment to foster this understanding is not easy. However, requiring students to set learning goals does help, as long as the activity includes an associated action plan to achieve the identified goals. The role of the teacher is to monitor their progress toward the goals and to advise on strategies, and provide evidence and resources to help students meet their goals. For example, teachers need to show students how assignments that satisfy incremental learning goals also feed into larger objectives and generic skills. One of the ways in which an e-portfolio assists this process is that it facilitates the process of students and assessors reviewing and discussing student work in the context of prior work, identified goals and earlier levels of goal achievement.

MY.ePortfolio website of Dalhousie University (n.d.) provides an excellent resource for students in how to set goals. The tips include: keeping goals positive, simple, measurable and specific. Goals should be set neither too high nor too low. The advice also confronts issues such as failures, obstacles and the need to change goals. This is the kind of resource students need in order to venture into the unfamiliar territory of assuming responsibility for their learning. The Dalhousie website (Figure 4.1) also gives advice on how to reach personal goals.

Regosin, Director of Academic Advising at St Lawrence University (SLU), outlines a process of goal setting for students across the whole undergraduate programme. The strategy begins with an 'exploratory

Dalhousie University: Tips for Writing Goals

Stay positive
Keep it simple
Focus on performance
Don't set your goals too high
Or too low
Measurable and specific
Changing your goals
Dealing with failure
Facing obstacles

Figure 4.1 Setting goals
Source: http://channelcontent.dal.ca/portfolio/sm_writegoals.html

goals' essay which students write during the advising period for registration in the summer before entering the university.

> This essay in its nature is an attempt on the students' part to seek the sources of their academic interests and where those coincide with courses and programs offered to them at SLU. Writing this essay is not simply a matter of rehearsing a personal statement from a college application. Rather, writing the exploratory essay is the means or the process by which students will come to know why they want to be here.
>
> (Regosin, n.d.)

Towards the end of their first year, students revise their exploratory essay by reflecting on the initial goals they set for themselves and assessing the relevance of those goals in the light of their experiences and who they have become in the intervening time. The third assignment requires students to consider why they have chosen a particular major and to offer a rationale for their choice. The aim is that students engage intentionally with their choice of subjects. The final step in the process involves students writing a formal proposal for a project to carry out in their fourth year in consultation with their faculty mentor. The proposal should address the following issues: their current interests and enthusiasms, any co-curricular activities that might be relevant, a reflection on the initial essay as well as a rationale for the way in which the project will provide a culmination of their programme of study at the university. Regosin notes:

One of the most powerful contributions any adviser can make is simply to encourage each student, as early as possible, to make connections between what goes on inside and outside of class. Advisors play a critical role in this context because most students don't think of making the connections themselves.

(Regosin, n.d.)

Individual e-portfolios may easily become the means by which a job seeker demonstrates what they can bring to a job. For the students, learning how to set personal learning outcomes as well as the strategies and performance indicators to meet them is a skill many employers will value. However the (over)use of the term 'e-portfolio' can place too much emphasis on the technology rather than on the generic skills developed by students through the use of an e-portfolio. Goal setting is such a skill and the activities around the process should emphasise both academic learning and personal experiences.

Peer and self-assessment

A third generic skill, closely associated with both reflection and goal setting, is the ability to assess one's own work as well as the work of one's peers. Other online learning technologies such as discussion boards provide a similar facility to e-portfolios in enabling peer commenting, but the advantage of an e-portfolio is that the commenting and self-assessment can be integrated directly with the student work. The aim of peer and self-assessment is to provide opportunities for students to develop reflective and critical thinking skills, the ability to evaluate and provide thoughtful responses to different points of view, and techniques they can use to encourage and support the work of other students. These skills also enhance students' ease with setting goals for themselves.

One way of introducing self-assessment is to require students to identify their current skill level at the beginning of a course. This exercise should include a list of actions needed to develop the areas in which they perceive themselves to be weak. Towards the end of the course this self-assessment should be reviewed and a further assessment made of skills acquired along with evidential statements to support their claims.

Self-assessment is often combined with peer assessment. A rubric is usually supplied by the teacher, encouraging students to address the quality of the work, the presentation, and strength of evidence. Students use the rubric to write an assessment of their own work as well as the work of one or two of their peers. In some cases of campus-based courses, the e-portfolio work is combined with a class presentation in which each student presents their portfolio and makes an oral report of their work.

A major benefit, recognised wherever peer assessment is used, is that students gain a valuable insight into how their own work is marked and in particular how marking criteria are used and how they can be aligned to learning objectives.

Peer commenting on student work is an excellent incentive for improving the quality and effort that students invest in their work. Furthermore, those who comment learn as much from devising their comments as those who receive the feedback on their work. Some practitioners divide students into groups of about four, each with access to the others' e-portfolios. This enables students to learn not only from reading each others' work, but also from seeing the feedback from the teacher and other students on that work. By comparing their own responses with the teacher's responses, students' ability to improve their own work is enhanced. They develop a greater capacity to identify weaknesses in their own work and to identify strategies for how and what to revise.

Communication skills

Communication skills are the foundation of all the generic skills discussed so far. Teachers who have used other forms of online communication have recognised the benefit of a real audience for students' written work. Instead of producing material for the teacher alone, students are suddenly writing for their peers. This usually has a very positive effect on the quality of work students produce. Sabre uses an e-portfolio approach to give students access to the work of previous students as well as to the portfolios-in-process of the current students. This helped to create an 'e-portfolio culture' (Sabre, 2002).

Most e-portfolio software allows others not only to view the student's work, but also to comment on it. Some systems have integrated synchronous and asynchronous communication processes with the e-portfolio software so that students can develop a group portfolio or can communicate with each other about a piece of work. In this sense, e-portfolios have developed well beyond a simple document storage facility in which students demonstrate their skills. As with electronic learning environments, e-portfolios can be used to actually develop student skills.

Peer commenting or assessing is one such application; another process facilitated by e-portfolios is mentoring. A number of teachers have noted that while providing advice and guidance to students throughout the course via their e-portfolios may seem to be a very time consuming activity, this is offset by the speed with which they can mark the final e-portfolio submission, as they are already familiar with the work. The on-going communication process between the student and the teacher or mentor about the goals, reflections and activities can be invaluable as a means of increasing students' understanding of their own learning.

E-portfolios have also been used specifically to develop communication skills. For example, students work in small teams to conduct internet research on a particular topic or problem. They create a joint document describing technical or factual information needed to address the issue. In addition they identify three critical questions or perspectives on the problem. Finally, they assess themselves in terms of teamwork and communication skills. This exercise brings together a range of learning processes: communication strategies about roles in a team, synergies, conflicts and conflict resolution issues.

Beyond a repository of information

The communication element of e-portfolio software begins to blur the boundary between an ELE and an e-portfolio, especially when the latter is used for group work. The essence of both these tools, however, is that they elevate students from mere consumers of knowledge to contributors and creators of knowledge. This takes place through the linking together of people, ideas, resources and experiences (Tosh and Werdmuller, 2005).

Activities centred around e-portfolio building could involve the following processes:

- Defining a problem or issue and developing a structure for approaching it
- Applying abstract theories to practice and vice versa
- Contextualising knowledge from one situation to another
- Making sense of disaggregated sources of information and knowledge
- Evaluating the quality, relevance or efficacy of information.

(From Graham, 2005)

As these processes are applied to specific curriculum areas, students will begin to appreciate their e-portfolio as a tool for learning. If the focus of the e-portfolio use is largely on assessment and accountability, students soon cease to engage with the lifelong learning promise and view it purely as a requirement for getting a degree.

Many course designers also use e-portfolio activities to integrate informal and non-formal learning experiences into the formal accreditation process. Recognising different forms of learning from a variety of contexts including the workplace and the home, is part of this inclusive view of learning. One practitioner notes:

> This is not as simple a task as might be at first assumed. Within the formal education system learning has been conflated with achievement. Although it could be said that all learning is an achievement it does not follow that the formal education system has recognised it as such. Learners frequently lack the skills to recognise their own learning, especially on-going learning which does not necessarily lead to formal outcomes.
>
> (Graham, 2005, p.121)

Moving e-portfolio use beyond an assessment tool or repository of work requires a design involving multiple connection points: for example formative submissions and comments from peers and mentors. Gathercoal *et al.* confirm this advice by underlining the critical importance of the faculty understanding their role as ongoing mentors, conveyors of standards and definers of quality (Gathercoal *et al.,* 2002).

Changing curriculum design

One of the more interesting observations to emerge from the use of e-portfolios in curriculum design is the way in which they are subtly altering the curriculum. This is the result of two factors:

1   The processes of student reflection provide the teacher with insight into which aspects of the curriculum are successful and which are not.
2   The public nature of e-portfolios, as with the web in general, means that teachers' curriculum design is subject to greater scrutiny – by their peers, potential student employers, outside experts etc.

Sabre's experience is typical:

> I continue to adjust the course based on feedback from the portfolios. In addition, the integration of portfolios into [the course] has

really helped get students out of playing 'the student game'. That is, they appear to place less energy into merely looking for the 'right answer' and spend more time reflecting on their experiences, synthesizing and postulating a new stance as a result. By using portfolios, our students are getting a sense of the bigger picture – and they can articulate what it is they believe and provide evidence to support these beliefs. The portfolio has helped to give them the framework for doing this.

(Sabre, 2002)

The public nature of e-portfolios has a positive effect on both the student and the teacher.

Many teachers share their students' e-portfolios as part of faculty development, and in cases of large classes with multiple markers, as a way of moderating the marking process. The electronic facility makes it easier to discuss comparable assignments, changes for subsequent years and weaknesses in the current curriculum. This is particularly important where courses involve interdisciplinary teaching and learning.

As e-portfolio use gains momentum, the curricula will increasingly be scrutinised by persons both in and out of academia, and will inevitably evolve to meet wider expectations. Business, industry, the arts, and government may influence and shape what is to be taught and assessed. In this sense, e-portfolios are not only tools for assessing learning and teaching, but more importantly they promote reform of the traditional educational system, and bridge the divide between the academy and society.

Summary and online resources

Too often, discussion about the general instructional nature of electronic portfolios is reduced to two distinct roles: portfolios as a means of assessing specific student performance, and portfolios as a showcase for demonstrating student accomplishments. In this chapter we have tried to indicate ways in which e-portfolios can be used as part of the learning process. The student-centred approach advocated here aims to develop reflective learners who explore their experiences of learning to better understand how they learn and how to improve their learning. E-portfolio processes can be used to promote generic, lifelong learning skills.

Penn State University reflection advice, online at: <http://eportfolio. psu.edu/build/reflect/reflect2.html>.

Richards, C. (2005) ICT integration, e-portfolios, and learning as an activity-reflection cycle, Teaching and Learning Forum, online at: <http://lsn.curtin.edu.au/tlf/tlf2005/refereed/richards.html>.

Higdon, J. and Tran, T. (2005) ePortfolios for reflective learning, USC Center for Learning, online at: <Http://www.educause.edu/ir/library/pdf /WRC0563. pdf>.

Center for Innovative Course Design, online at: <http://www.cicd.neu.edu/news _and_events/?id=22>.

Online case studies

Ford, D., Harley, P. and Smallwood, A. (2004) 'Integrating an eportfolio within a university and the wider community', workshop presentation, EIfEL ePortfolio Conference, La Rochelle, October 2004, online at: <http://www.nottingham.ac.uk/eportfolio/specifyinganeportfolio/keydocu-ments/LaRochellePaper.doc>.

Cotterill, S., McDonald, R., Drummond, P. and Hammond, G. (2004) 'Design, implementation and evaluation of a "generic" ePortfolio: the Newcastle experience', Paper presented at the ePortfolio Conference 2004, La Rochelle, online at: <www.eportfolios.ac.uk/FDTL4/docs>.

Love, D., McKean, G. & Gathercoal, P. (2004) 'Portfolios to webfolios and beyond: levels of maturation', Educause Quarterly, 27 (2), online at: <http://www.educause.edu/apps/eq/eqm04/eqm0423.asp>.

Vuorikari, R. (2006) Portfolios in teacher training – national policies and case studies. Europortfolio 2005, Cambridge, UK, online at: <http://insight. eun.org/shared/data/insight/documents/e_portfolio_teacher_training_final_1 0_05.pdf>.

Stefani, L. (n.d.). 'PDP/CPD and e-portfolios: rising to the challenge of modelling good practice, online at: <http:www.alt.ac.uk/docs/lorraine_stefani_ paper.doc>.

West Cheshire College Electronic NVQ case study, n.d., Becta, online at: <http://ferl.becta.org.uk/display.cfm?resID=13052&printable =1>.

Tosh, D., Light, T. Fleming, K. and Haywood, J. (2005) 'Engagement with electronic portfolios: challenges from the student perspective', Canadian Journal of Learning and Technology 31(3), online at: <http:// www.cjlt.ca/content/vol31.3/tosh.html>.

Irvin, L. (2005). 'Reflection in the Electronic Writing Classroom.' Computers and Composition Online. 26 Dec. 2005. http://www.bgsu.edu/cconline/irvin/ Importance.htm.

Chapter 5

E-portfolios and assessment of student learning

Assessment of student learning is a taxing issue for all teachers in further and higher education, with a range of factors to be taken into consideration. First and foremost is the importance of ensuring alignment between the intended learning outcomes and the assessment strategies. Does the assessment plan cover the knowledge, skills and understanding encompassed within the course? Increasingly there is a need to consider the assessment load, both for students and for staff, particularly in the context of large classes of students. There is also the need to take into account both formative and summative assessment. Chapter 4 emphasised the importance of moving beyond using the e-portfolio as a repository and a simple tool for assessment. It also highlighted the need to review and revise curriculum design to reflect a shifting teaching and learning paradigm encompassing increased use of technology. Assessment of student learning in an electronic environment presents us with some new challenges in how we conceptualise assessment of student learning.

In different learning contexts there will be different stated purposes for the e-portfolio and there may also be significant shifts over a period of time. This chapter will explore assessment and expand upon some of the potential tensions relating to assessment using e-portfolios.

Linking assessment and e-portfolio purpose

The importance of clarifying the purpose of the e-portfolio cannot be overstated. This will also help to define aspects of the assessment strategy, and the approach to teaching and learning. In Chapter 3 a list of different types of portfolio was presented. That list included:

- *The showcase portfolio* – a portfolio that is publicly accessible and is essentially a demonstration of student work.

- *The development portfolio* – a portfolio that shows work in progress and identifies the student's development needs and progress. This portfolio can be the basis of discussion with the tutor or supervisor.
- *The reflective portfolio* – intended to enable students to assess their own growth and changes in their thinking over a period of time. This may be a purely personal portfolio.
- *The assessment portfolio* – a portfolio used as part of the assessment strategy. Here documents and other artefacts are collected primarily for the purpose of assessment, although they could subsequently be used for other purposes.

These different types of e-portfolio can each play a different role in assessment. They may impact on assessment to a greater or lesser extent. If, for example, the main purpose of the portfolio is as a showcase of an individual student's work, there may be no need to alter the assessment strategy significantly. The real benefit to students of having this style of portfolio may be in how they present themselves in job applications or in interviews. Students can be encouraged to work with career counsellors to find the best ways of presenting their achievements or aligning their skills with job or career goals. They will benefit from feedback from their tutor and peers, but the academic reader is not the primary audience. The language used and the emphasis given in the content will be focused on the external audience. Students pulling together a showcase e-portfolio may be encouraged to be highly creative and see this as a 'fun' activity to record and present their achievements. Novelty may well be attractive to employers and ensure that their e-portfolio is noticed above others. The standards on which a showcase e-portfolio is judged may not be academic ones.

If the e-portfolio is more aligned with personal development and personal development planning (PDP), there could well be an expectation that the student will build their e-portfolio throughout their college or university career. This provides an opportunity for the student to document their development as well as their final achievement. This type of e-portfolio calls for fresh thinking on how the curriculum is designed and on the changing roles and responsibilities of teachers and students. This is not a new idea. Educators such as Stefani and Nicol (1997), Barnett (1994) and Elton (2003) have been writing about the shifting roles of teachers and learners for many years. It takes time for the rhetoric to turn into reality in colleges and universities. The digital world might just be the catalyst needed to significantly change thinking in this respect. As courses become more personalised, and each student follows a different 'pattern' rather than a standard course, the development e-portfolio becomes more important. It directly addresses the wider choices that students now have to make.

If the student 'e-portfolio space' is linked with the electronic learning environment (e.g. Blackboard, WebCT, Moodle, etc.) then students will have access to full records of their performance on both formative and summative assessments. Students can archive this information in their portfolio, thus supporting and encouraging personal development planning activities, particularly as students mature in their learning and begin to think about career options.

In the reflective e-portfolio students can choose to expose and reflect on a range of completed work, but may also choose to retain some of their reflection as a personal and private resource. Some academic activity will require students to reflect on their progress at key points over the duration of a course or programme of study. It may even be a course requirement (part of the assessment) that they complete the e-portfolio, but this need not imply 'showcase' quality. With a reflective e-portfolio, even if some work is flawed, students may be encouraged to include it. Incomplete work can still illustrate how far the student has progressed. Students may choose to include planning documents, failed experiments and 'test pieces' for the same reason.

The 'assessment portfolio' may in itself constitute a major aspect of the learning and assessment strategy. In that case the process of developing the e-portfolio is something on which the students will be assessed as well as the products within it. Both Veugelers *et al.* (2004) and Elton (2003) suggest that e-portfolios are well suited to the idea of authentic learning and authentic assessment. Elton argues that students should be assessed on their performance as this relates to their potential. Using negotiated learning agreements, this work could be presented in an e-portfolio with students choosing the work to be presented on the basis of a self-evaluation. Veugelers *et al.* believe that portfolios should be part of the student learning contract and that to be successful with e-portfolios requires a reconsideration of the curriculum and the overall student learning experience.

As these examples show, the introduction of e-portfolios – as with all other learning activity – requires us to be clear about what it is we are assessing. The student e-portfolio can have different purposes within the assessment process. As these different purposes are founded on different pedagogic approaches, they will result in portfolios with different characteristics. Trying to use a single portfolio to bridge multiple purposes could be detrimental to student learning and also create challenges for assessment. For example if students understand the portfolio to be for the purpose of reflection and development, but in fact it is also to be used for summative assessment, they may feel more restricted in what they put into their portfolio. They could become risk averse and less creative in their choices and presentation.

Helen Barrett, a strong advocate for e-portfolios, comments that a 'portfolio whose purpose is to foster learning and document growth over time is based upon a constructivist model of learning' (Barrett and Carney, 2005). She suggests that portfolio authoring reflects the tenets of constructivism in that it allows for students to begin their learning at many different starting points. Formative feedback or critique challenges the student's original insights prompting reflection and revision. In this sense, the portfolio is a tool to support the process of learning, and assessment is formative. The portfolio becomes a 'story' of learning owned by the learner (Barrett and Carney, 2005; Acker, 2005).

Changing views on assessment

We must also be aware that any consideration of how e-portfolios 'fit' with assessment occurs during a period when views on assessment are also changing. Traditional approaches to assessment of student learning have been criticised for placing too much emphasis on transmitted knowledge. On-line assessment in general has been closely aligned with the objective of providing students with greater levels of flexibility and access in learning (James *et al.*, 2002). We now need to consider the emergence of new forms of assessment which may be particularly aligned with the use of e-portfolios. The trends that we will concentrate on in this chapter are *constructivism, authentic assessment* and *peer assessment.* We will also look at what e-portfolios offer for *self-assessment.*

Constructivism and e-portfolios

Jackson (Jackson, 2003), writing about the 'creative curriculum' suggests that it is time to move away from 'narrow, summatively driven' assessment practices and criteria that focus on what is known. He points out that these practices do not recognise the process of learning and how learners come to know. They do not, and cannot, recognise emergent unanticipated learning outcomes. He believes we should be encouraging students to construct new knowledge rather than to show how much of transmitted knowledge they have retained. This is a 'constructivist' view, one which is very important in teaching and learning currently. This pedagogical approach is one which is frequently associated with e-learning.

Authentic assessment

In recent years there has also been much more emphasis on the idea of authentic assessment. Authentic assessment is defined by Herman *et al.* (1992) as 'variants of performance assessments that require students to generate rather than choose a response' (p.12). Elton and Johnston (2002) see authentic assessment as testing a learner's ability to carry out activities that resemble authentic situations. It implies improvements in the relevance of learning and assessment. In conventional or traditional assessment strategies there may have been a tendency to prepare students for specific, sometimes rather artificial, tests. This can translate into a narrowing of the curriculum. The teaching becomes focused on passing the test rather than offering learners a relevant and appropriate curriculum. It has been argued that authentic assessment offers something substantially different. It can be transformative, setting up learning situations which encourage the creation of new knowledge (Elton, 2003; O'Suilleabhain, 2004).

Authentic assessment must be built upon authentic learning experiences. The e-portfolio can be helpful here in recording that authentic learning, by allowing students to compile different kinds of evidence of learning. For example there is the capability to use text, audio, video clips, and 3D graphics as well as photographic evidence and other forms of presentation. The opportunity for flexibility and creativity can enhance student learning and increase the potential for authentic self-evaluation and reflection on learning. Different types and forms of presentations within an e-portfolio can be viewed and assessed together as a structured collection. This allows for demonstration of development and reflection over time, and sometimes engagement with a wider audience using, for example, electronic commenting. Technology also increases the scope to update and upgrade versions of material. Using blogs, wikis or podcasts (see Chapter 9) can support the process of development and reflection, making the learning journal visible as well as showcasing the end-product.

Peer assessment

How far we go with the idea of peer assessment depends on the level and the complexity of the learning situation. Online media can support distributed collaborative interaction and dialogue as well as access to information and resources. E-portfolios can support the development of 'electronic communities' where the exchanges are visible and can be referenced and linked to. While there is still a long way to go to embed this type of learning into the curriculum in most colleges and universities, there are moves toward building and valuing 'electronic communities of learners' where peer review and comment are the focus of learning activity. Approaches that involve peer assessment are also likely to have some association with constructivist and authentic assessment approaches. They support authentic learning tasks and assessment (McConnell, 2000; Garrison and Anderson, 2003).

E-portfolios, formative assessment and student learning

Can an e-portfolio act as a vehicle for meaningful formative assessment? This question may well be key to the success of e-portfolio implementation. If we assume it can, we are also assuming that other conditions such as the purpose of e-portfolio implementation, the technological infrastructure to support e-portfolios and the course design considerations have been addressed.

We need to be careful that students don't see the portfolio as just another chore with no real value for them. Formative assessment can be associated with the student's reflection on their learning, with input by the teacher about the portfolio contents and construction. This approach gives the student a sense of ownership over their learning, supports independence and turns the e-portfolio into an active vehicle of learning (Johnston, 2004).

This issue is really one at the heart of teaching and learning using e-portfolios. Does the e-portfolio support a structured approach to learning? Will students recognise and repond to this? If students are given structured activities to enable them to practise participation in the learning process, this can facilitate the gradual building up of appropriate learning skills (Vygotsky, 1978). The e-portfolio can be an environment in which students can practise and on which they can receive useful feedback.

In any learning context, formative assessment is for the purpose of providing regular feedback to students to stimulate their learning and to provide them with information to judge the effectiveness of their learning strategies (Miller *et al.,* 1998). A major claim made in current literature is that formative assessment of portfolios can enable productive forms of learning to take place (Johnston, 2004). If we consider the types of formative assessment which can support student learning, they include:

- Self-assessment through the process of reflection and reporting on reflection with feedback from teachers and tutors.
- Peer assessment, which implies that there must be a sharing of information or allowing for work to be scrutinised/viewed by other students. Alternatively peer assessment can mean social interaction (using technology) and an encouragement for learners/peers to engage in dialogue on each other's work.
- Teacher/tutor led feedback or dialogue allowing for sharing of expertise between student and teacher, encouraging the student to progress their learning.

Some research (e.g. Ramsden, 2003; Biggs, 1999) suggests that students may not fully understand the importance of formative assessment, or how to respond to feedback on their learning. If the e-portfolio is viewed as a means to support students in reflecting on and evaluating their own learning, as would be the case if the portfolio is linked to personal development planning, there is an implicit notion that students are being encouraged to take more responsibility for their own learning. It becomes possible to formatively assess the processes of learning through intermediate products. Formative assessment in this sense would then really be used for its main purpose, to support students in closing the gap between current and hoped for achievement (Stefani, 1998). However we cannot take for granted, particularly in the earlier years of college or university level study, that students will understand the purpose of formative assessment. In fact we might want to consider changing the term altogether and uncouple it from the common student view of assessment – as a means of gaining a mark for their assignment.

Summative assessment and e-portfolios

There are many purposes associated with summative assessment, whether in a traditional setting or in an electronic environment. It covers, but moves beyond formative assessment in:

- grading students, and through this
- estimating students' learning potential. That information can be used for

- guiding students in course selection. In some cases this could require students to achieve a certain standard in summative assessment before proceeding with their studies.

As with formative assessment there are more general learning support aims:

- Providing feedback on student learning
- Motivating students to learn
- Consolidating the learning that is occurring
- Enabling students to apply abstract concepts to practical problems
- Providing feedback for academic staff on the effectiveness of their teaching
- Providing information for quality assurance purposes.

Unfortunately while it is possible to identify multiple purposes for assessment such as those mentioned above (Brown and Glasser, 1999), the range of methods actually deployed remains very limited.

One great hope for new learning and teaching technologies relates to their potential to allow a much greater level of creativity in teaching, learning and assessment. However this has not yet been realised. As Trehan and Reynolds (2002) observe: 'Examples of critical pedagogies including those situations on-line are accumulating, but they seldom exhibit corresponding changes in assessment practices' (p.280).

We would suggest that it is anomalous to encourage students to maintain e-portfolios, but then to fall back on tradition with regard to assessment of student learning. Instead we expect that use of e-portfolios is linked to integration of e-learning with classroom activities and assessment. On-line assessment, whether e-portfolio driven or otherwise, offers substantial advantages (Jenkins, 2004; James et al., 2002; Peat and Franklin, 2002). For example:

- Flexibility of access in time, place and the selection of assessment options.
- Equitability, taking into consideration diversity (e.g. international students).
- Reducing time constraints and allowing more opportunity for students to demonstrate their knowledge and understanding.
- Student-centred learning. Open access can encourage students to take responsibility for their own learning.

- Immediacy of feedback for students (if this is designed into the assessment).
- The potential for interactive assessment tasks that are more authentic and in themselves learning experiences. This could include online text questions that incorporate information-rich images, sound and text.
- Immediate reporting of marks and outcomes to staff for monitoring and adaptation.
- The potential to reduce costs and staff workloads through automation of routine assessment tasks.
- Enhancement of student learning outcomes which can lead to positive attitudes to learning.

Well designed online courses can incorporate a number of ways of providing both formative and summative feedback on student learning.

Gunn and Harper (2006) suggest some principles for providing online formative and summative feedback which is helpful to our thinking about assessment and e-portfolios:

- Provide accessible tools (hardware and networks) and mediate a commitment by students to use these tools. Students need usable tools and the skills and preparation to use them.
- Use online testing with explanations and feedback as a catalyst for students to attain mastery of their subject area. In e-portfolios commenting by fellow students, tutor or an external audience can serve this purpose.
- Incorporate corrective feedback to exploit the usefulness of errors as a means to address misconceptions and offer the benefits of immediate remedial instruction. In e-portfolios the use of wikis, blogs or podcasts (Chapter 9) can show the development of ideas and illustrate how corrective feedback has been acted on.
- Build rewards into a formative assessment structure to provide bridging motivation while students become committed to independently defined programmes of study. The e-portfolio has the potential to be a useful, usable and personal resource throughout the student's formal education and beyond.

These principles will work best if flexibility is a key to the course design. For example, will students be limited to on-campus access to the e-portfolio? Or can they access (upload and download) online 24/7? We should not assume that e-portfolios are some sort of 'magic bullet' to sort out assessment problems. They require thoughtful and thorough integration into assessment. Only in this way will students recognise their e-portfolio as a constructive learning tool and 'somewhere' to engage in reflection on their learning.

The problem of making assessment reliable

Some of the current literature and research on summative assessment, particularly in higher education, questions the emphasis that has been placed on 'reliability' of assessment. For example Elton (2003) argues that 'for too long assessment has been dominated by the demand for reliability above everything else'. What do we mean by 'reliability'? An accepted definition is: 'Reliability refers to the consistency of marks obtained by the same individuals when re-examined with the same test on different occasions, or with different sets of equivalent test items or under variable assessment conditions' (Bennett, 1993, p.89).

Elton suggests that conflating all individual assessments into a single number to give the final degree class or final grade for a course is inappropriate. He points out that this has resulted in a bias towards measuring that which is easy to measure rather than assessing more complex but desirable learning outcomes. Referring back to our earlier list of summative assessment functions we can see that these concentrate almost exclusively on grading. This approach is also questionable when we consider Jackson's views about unanticipated learning outcomes (Jackson, 2003). We are leaving little scope for creativity and diversity when we emphasise reliability above all. Elton (2003) suggests that while assessments must in the first place be valid in that they assess the declared learning outcomes, their reliability must be treated within the constraints of their validity. This gives prominence to whether the assessment is appropriate and meaningful and is concerned with its accuracy and replicability within that frame. Given Jackson's views we might also question a reliance in all circumstances on a narrow range of anticipated learning outcomes. The e-portfolio is likely to be an unusually extensive and complex assessment piece.

If authentic assessment strategies are used, and students are given more ownership over how they present their work, the flexibility provided by technology means that they should be producing very different e-portfolios. They will differ from our set of expectations and be different from each other. The ability to accurately and consistently grade diverse, highly complex student pieces, is then brought into question. Work by Baume and Yorke (2002) on conventional but complex portfolios suggests that consistent grading of e-portfolio assessments could be very problematic, with different markers coming to very different opinions. This in turn links with the issue of assessment criteria. Students are able to be more creative in how they learn, how they organise their portfolio and in the types of materials or artefacts they present. This could mean that no two students can be assessed on precisely the same criteria, particularly if it is the evidence of the learning process (which the portfolio allows for), as well as the final product of learning that is being assessed. This learning process may have been individually negotiated and could be highly personalised.

One solution may be to include students more actively in the assessment process. We might also consider using more self- and peer-assessment strategies. Just as the assessment 'product' is more individual, so is the assessment process itself a negotiation between staff and students on the assessment criteria for certain tasks. (Self- and peer-assessment issues are discussed again in the next section.)

Another approach is to move away from grades. Elton (2003) believes we should: 'grade what can be assessed validly and reliably bearing in mind that there are learning outcomes we should value that cannot be assessed both validly and reliably. Where there are assessments that can be assessed validly but not reliably then we should grade as pass/fail and not try to convert into a percentage mark.'

Students as well as staff may be uncomfortable with this. Taking it further, Elton expresses the view that instead of a degree classification, we should be moving towards profiling. This is compatible with the idea of the e-portfolio as it links with personal development planning and lifelong learning. Reform along these lines has recently been suggested in the UK (Burgess, 2005), but it may take some time for that view to be accepted and for change to be implemented.

Returning to e-portfolios, Falchikov (2005) presents one rubric for judging a portfolio which was developed by Birchenbaum using a four-point scale (Table 5.1).

Although these guidelines were developed to apply to paper-based portfolios, they could obviously be adapted to e-portfolios. This scheme shows how very different e-portfolios could be assessed and avoids the use of spuriously precise grades or marks.

Courses which are already established in their use of portfolios, for example many UK-based Postgraduate Certificates in Learning and Teaching in Higher Education, may already be choosing to assess portfolios as 'Achieved', 'Well achieved' or 'Not yet achieved' in relation to learning outcomes, rather than attempting to grade them more finely.

These judgements are reached within the type of assessment approach advocated by Challis (1999):

- assessment should be carried out within a criterion referenced framework
- criteria should be explicit and understood by staff and students
- assessment criteria should be linked to specific learning outcomes
- evidence of learning should be accompanied by explanatory reflective statements
- evidence must be authentic, appropriate to demonstrate the learning claimed and recent or current enough for the assessor to infer that learning is ongoing.

Table 5.1 A four-point scale for judging a portfolio

4 points	*3 points*	*2 points*	*1 point*
Entries carefully chosen to give picture of a reflective learner, what learner knows and can do and progress made. Entries bear relationship to each other and to a central organising theme. Rationale for choices clearly stated and reflects well grounded self-assessment. Student aware of audience's perspectives.	Evidence of thought regarding choice of entries. Each justified and reflected upon. More and less effective entries compared. Student aware of own learning process. Some evidence of reflection. BUT Portfolio lacks a central purpose, and entries do not create a coherent picture. Insufficient evidence of awareness of audience perspectives.	Some evidence of intentional selection. Some evidence of reflection. BUT Reasons for selection shallow (e.g. 'I liked it'). Portfolio lacks organising theme/central purpose. Not enough evidence to build picture of student as a learner.	Portfolio is haphazard collection. No evidence of intentional selection of entries. No comparisons between entries or organisation according to central theme. No picture of student as reflective learner suggested.

Source: Falchikov, 2005

Self and peer assessment

If the portfolio is seen as a tool that allows for the storing, documentation, updating and selection of students' work, then it is possible to allow students to put forward for assessment work that is chosen by them to show their positive achievements.

Self- and peer-assessment strategies are an important part of the process of encouraging students to make choices and take more responsibility for and ownership of their learning. Part of our role as educators is to help students develop the skills to make objective judgements on their own and others' work. We can, fortunately, draw on a vast body of literature on encouraging and implementing self- and peer-assessment strategies for a range of learning tasks (see for example Boud, 1995, Falchikov, 2005).

As students mature in their learning they will be able to exercise more control. They may use different aspects of their e-portfolio to demonstrate what they can do, what they cannot yet do, and what they intend to do, based on their self-assessment or self-evaluation against personal learning goals and their progress towards those goals.

The e-portfolio can be supported by online self-assessment opportunities. For example in the Engineering Faculty at the University of Auckland, a program has been developed that has short engineering/mathematical problems. Students can access this any time, any place and gain instant feedback. The program allows students to assess how they are doing and gain useful insights into areas they may need to study further. The questions are randomised to dissuade memorisation and encourage deeper learning. Experiences with this type of self-assessment could be noted in the e-portfolio. A development e-portfolio could direct the student to periodically test and review their understanding through self-assessment. Multiple choice tests are an obvious means of encouraging self-assessment, sometimes used as a diagnostic tool, to promote the idea that students can pinpoint areas where they need to engage in further study.

E-portfolios can also support new approaches to peer assessment. For example, it is possible to set up group projects for students, negotiate an assignment and ask the student groups to present individual reports on their project processes and products, which are commented on by that group and others. Students through email, discussion boards and online bulletin boards build an iterative exchange of ideas, collaborative learning and peer assessment and feedback. A more formal peer assessment approach could use a web-based form to structure comments and feedback. With either approach, the e-portfolio then becomes an effective tool for students to modify, share and exchange learning resources (Stefani, 2005). This is the type of peer learning/peer feedback situation advocated by Collis (2005) in providing authentic learning situations for distance learners.

With any group work assessment, there is always an issue with managing the assessment of the individual in the context of the group. In an electronic environment there is a clearer 'audit trail' that tutors and teachers can use to monitor online communication to determine the extent of individual student contributions. Another way around this is to encourage the students themselves to negotiate their way through this as part of the group learning process.

Case example: Learning objects and e-portfolios, a question of choice

Before leaving the subject of assessment it is worth considering an example from The Open University which shows how an e-portfolio approach may be used in a course where students have a high degree of autonomy in choosing how and what content they study. The course, Learning in the Connected Economy, is an online postgraduate course within an established masters programme. It is unusual in providing content as a set of learning objects and allowing students to make choices between these, in terms of what they study, when they study and – very often – how they study. A fresh assessment approach was needed to reflect this exceptional level of student choice. It asked students to produce a commentary which referred to and accompanied an electronic portfolio of evidence. This portfolio was a purposeful selection of eight learning objects from a possible 'long list' of 55 across the course. The quality of the selection (its appropriateness) was part of the marking criteria and many students reported initial problems with the idea of making choices, typically wishing to use more than eight items. However, two-thirds of the students reported very positively on the assessment approach. The feedback from students on the course reflected their background as e-learning practitioners. They were well aware of the issues and showed clear understanding of the implications of using an e-portfolio. For example, as one reflected:

> The e-portfolio was a big step towards affirming what we had learned – it brought together some of the work we had done during the course and forced us to reflect and link these LOs [learning objects] together.

Pedagogically this is very sound. It allowed us to individualise our final piece of work, which considering the groups were made up of diverse interests (teachers, designers, managers etc) was very important and very clever. It also allowed those of us who had not looked at every LO to hand in a complete work. Those that had looked at more LOs than others would hopefully be at an advantage.

(Mason *et al.*, 2004, p.725)

Although this implementation of e-portfolios did not use a specific e-portfolio system and was limited by the range of the evidence, it did suggest to the course authors that it would be problematic to assess a course with this degree of student choice *without* using an electronic portfolio.

The difference an e-portfolio makes

Using their e-portfolio, students may be asked to upload traditional assignments such as essays for marking. However technology allows us to be much more sophisticated if we choose. It gives us the potential to create connected documents with links to other sources. It allows us to incorporate multiple media. The e-portfolio encourages fresh thinking about assessment and further consideration of the issue of assessment based on authentic learning experiences, constructivist learning approaches and the role of peers as assessors. Projects or case studies investigating 'real world issues' could result in all students presenting very different work based on individual or group research. Each e-portfolio could be substantially different, in format, appearance *and* content. Using e-portfolio in assessment encourages students to be creative, and this creativity may in turn challenge conventional assessment – particularly summative assessment. If students are to be asked to present their portfolio for formal assessment, it is worth considering how the students themselves could be included and involved in setting the criteria by which they will be assessed.

This chapter has outlined a range of considerations relating to assessment in the context of e-learning and e-portfolios. As yet there are not many published examples of assessment using e-portfolios and those that exist are generally based on areas such as nursing or teaching, or follow the longer-term trend of use of showcase assessment portfolios in art and architecture.

Taken with Chapter 4 on course design we hope we have now given the reader an insight into some new e-portfolio-friendly approaches to course and curriculum design. We have considered how student learning can be facilitated through use of e-portfolios and how to devise workable strategies for assessment of student assessment using e-portfolios.

Finishing with an example based on teaching with learning objects shows how the personalised approach of the e-portfolio can work with one of the newer approaches to course design within e-learning. In the future, we may find in a range of subjects that e-portfolios are the logical way to provide summative assessment. E-portfolios have already been proven, in paper-based form, to have usefulness for formative assessment.

The website for this book and the list of URLs at the end of the book are intended to help readers to keep abreast of current developments in e-portfolios. They include links to information about e-portfolios and assessment.

Chapter 6

The e-portfolio as a tool for professional development

While the previous chapters have emphasised the importance of encouraging student responsibility for learning and promoting the concept of reflection on learning, often one of the barriers to progress is lack of a modelling by staff of the processes involved in reflection and of developing and maintaining a portfolio.

Over the past decade or so there has been an increasing emphasis especially within Higher Education on teaching portfolios – and more recently an emphasis on e-teaching portfolios. Many of the issues that relate to e-portfolios for students apply equally to e-portfolios for staff. There is anecdotal evidence to suggest that one of the barriers to staff developing and maintaining an e-portfolio is that there has been a lack of appropriate structures and templates for e-portfolios and a lack of professional development opportunities targeted to this aspect of scholarship. This chapter attempts to address some of these points by providing a synthesis of the recent literature on teaching portfolios with an emphasis later in the chapter on developments in e-portfolios for teaching staff using a current example of an e-teaching portfolio framework.

Some considerations for teachers in colleges and universities are that they are often working within a highly complex environment, under serious resource constraints and with growing demands being made on them relating to quality assurance and accountability, thus increasing levels of pressure particularly for university lecturers to be highly competitive in traditional research publication and the potentially competing demand to provide an effective and efficient learning experience for a growing population of students.

While many teaching and teaching-related staff may wish to argue the point on this, even for research-led universities, the overriding purpose of universities is not in fact to be research institutes, albeit that research is a high-order function of universities. Rather, the purpose of universities is to make use of and link research into teaching the student population.

If we interrogate the teaching function of universities, our responsibilities include: the development of students' critical abilities; the development of students' autonomy; supporting the student's character formation; and presentation and enhancement of society's intellectual culture (Barnett, 1994). This list of responsibilities applies as much to Further Education Colleges as it does to universities and is part and parcel of our commitment to supporting lifelong learning.

With the policies of expansion of higher/tertiary education, these latter responsibilities can seem a tall order. The student population is more diverse and in a competitive world learners' priorities may have changed to simply 'getting a good degree or other qualification to get a well paid job' (Knight, 2002).

The knowledge explosion as a result of the World Wide Web and of course the potential of communications and information technology do add further pressures on to teaching staff. If we are trying to encourage our students to use ICT, we do have some responsibility to upskill ourselves in this respect.

Stefani and Elton (2002) argue that to support the professional development of teachers in colleges and universities it is important to convince them that their teaching is a problematic activity worthy of reflection and research, and to enable them to engage in such activities. One means of doing this is to encourage and promote professional development through initiating and maintaining a teaching portfolio.

The aim of this chapter is to consider the teaching portfolio as a tool to support reflection on teaching activities, the transition from paper-based folios to e-folios and to summarise the potential for professional development related to teaching embedded within the idea of the teaching portfolio.

The link between learning and teaching portfolios

Possibly one of the best publications on portfolios for teaching staff is Peter Seldin's book *The Teaching Portfolio: A Practical Guide to Improved Performance and Promotion/Tenure Decisions* (1997), in which he outlines the advantages and benefits arising from the process of creating and maintaining teaching portfolios. He sees the advantages as including:

- the opportunity, through the process of preparation of a teaching portfolio, for considered reflection on one's teaching objectives and means of delivery;
- assistance in both professional development and personal growth;
- a means of providing a formal and verifiable record of teaching accomplishment that can be used for a variety of vocational and personnel purposes including continuation/tenure review, salary review, promotion, applications for leave, work unit balance and professional development generally;
- provision of a tool or measure to assist in assessing applications for teaching awards or prizes.

If we compare the points above with the student portfolio being promoted by Stanford University Learning Laboratory it is not difficult to see the parallels between personal development planning (PDP) issues for students and continuing professional development (CPD) for staff.

The purpose of the Stanford University e-folio is to support individual students to capture, organise, integrate and reuse the results of their formal and informal learning experiences over time, as well as to allow students to take advantage of this accumulated information to plan and assess the progress of their learning career with peers, faculty advisors and future employers.

There are moves globally for reform of teaching practices in colleges and universities. There has been a growing tendency towards greater accountability from teachers and an expectation that they will be able to provide clear and concise evidence of the quality of their classroom teaching.

It has often been the case that promotions and tenure committees are provided with little factual information about teaching performance. It has been seen as an easier option to provide information about publications, research grants and other scholarly accomplishments than to provide actual evidence of good or excellent teaching (Seldin, 1997).

While a teaching portfolio may be described as 'a factual description of one's teaching strengths and achievements', it can also be used to contribute to more sound decisions on promotion and tenure and to the professional development and growth of individual staff members. Those points also parallel some of the benefits of portfolios for students. The teaching portfolio, as well as providing a factual record, can also include documentation and resource materials that give an indication of the scope and quality of one's teaching performance.

According to Seldin (1997) the teaching portfolio can serve multiple purposes which include:

- a 'live' document for reflecting on how one's teaching has evolved over time
- preparation of materials on teaching effectiveness when applying for a new position or probation/continuation review
- sharing expertise and experience with younger staff members
- applying for teaching awards or grants relating to teaching
- leaving behind a 'portfolio' of selected materials so that future generations of teachers who will be taking over teaching courses will gain insights and experience.

On their Faculty and Teaching Associate Development website Ohio State University express the function of a teaching portfolio as follows:

- It is a way to collect evidence of your teaching ability
- It provides the reader with a context for your teaching
- It provides summary data on your teaching in a simple readable format
- It is focussed on quality, not quantity
- It is an organized record and its various sections relate to each other
- It is an ever-changing, evolving, live document
- It allows for self-reflection
- It provides an opportunity to be unique and showcase your personal style of teaching
- The process of creating a portfolio is generally much more important and meaningful than the end product.

To develop a teaching portfolio as a tool for reflection and as a tool to enable presentation of evidence of current practice requires:

a) A definition of 'portfolio' which can be contextualised for the roles and responsibilities of individual faculty.
b) Indicators or pointers to how individuals might construct their portfolio.
c) Inbuilt guidance as to how the portfolio can be maintained as a 'live' document for formative self-development, scholarly and evaluative purposes, rather than as a tailored summative instrument to be used for formal institutional purposes such as confirmation in post (continuation), promotion, salary review, etc.

A simple 'Google' search will bring up many thousands of references on teaching portfolios and some of these resources have been included at the end of this chapter. The teaching portfolio is being used so commonly in colleges and universities in the United States, Canada, Australia and the UK that it is now possible to provide a summary of the sorts of items most commonly accumulated within the portfolio. The next section will highlight the common components.

What goes into a teaching portfolio?

Because a teaching portfolio is unique to the individual, no two portfolios look alike. For teaching staff, it is worth bearing this in mind when considering the learning portfolio. Just as we might want our individuality and creativity to be apparent in our portfolios, so too will our students want to feel that they can individualise their portfolio to give it personal meaning.

Which items you choose to include in your portfolio will depend on the type of teaching you carry out, your academic discipline, your purpose for the folio and your intended audience. Seldin (1997) suggests that portfolio items might fall into three categories – material from oneself; material from others; the products of teaching/student learning. Unpackaging these broad categories, items potentially to be included within each category are listed below.

Material from oneself

- A statement on teaching philosophy. There is much anecdotal evidence to reveal that teaching staff often find it difficult to articulate their teaching philosophy. This could be compared with students finding it difficult to express their learning styles and strategies or their learning goals. There is clearly an abundance of educational jargon which can be piled up and used in vaguely appropriate ways in a 'teaching philosophy statement'. However, if this jargon is not backed up by evidence, it is rendered meaningless. For example the mission statements of many colleges or universities will claim that there is a student-centred or learner-centred ethos within the institution. Rarely though is there any explanation of what this means in practice. Likewise terms such as student-centred or learner-centred could be used in a teaching statement by an individual – but such terminology needs to be backed up by examples of what one means by 'student-centred'. The same thing applies to terms such as 'deep and surface learning' – if you hope to engender deep learning, what are you actually doing in your class to achieve this, how are you assessing your students to place an emphasis on deep learning as opposed to surface learning or memorisation? Your teaching philosophy should link very closely with other materials in your portfolio. The teaching philosophy statement might also include clear descriptions of your teaching strategies, objectives and methodologies.

- Statements of teaching responsibilities. To personalise these, it is important to contextualise the information. Include course titles and numbers, enrolments, perhaps some information on the characteristics of your student groups e.g. gender balance, ethnicity, students with English as an additional language (EAL); statements on whether the course is mandatory for the students enrolled or an elective subject, postgraduate or undergraduate.
- Course planning outlines, sample course syllabus giving a reasonable overview of course content, objectives, teaching methods, course learning resources, reading, assignments. When archiving such material in your portfolio, it will be useful to show it to colleagues to ascertain whether there would be sufficient information for someone else to pick up the course at short notice if need be.
- Participation in professional development opportunities relating to teaching and learning. It is not unusual to see teaching portfolios in which the owner/author has provided a list of professional development workshops attended. This is very superficial because it gives no indication of whether attendance at workshops/seminars was merely to satisfy an institutional 'rule' or condition or whether the professional development event was chosen for a particular reason and whether or not it had any impact on your approach to teaching.
- Indication of any revisions you have made for the curriculum, new course projects, updating of materials or class assignments, innovations you implemented into the class and how these impacted on your students.
- Evidence of teaching effectiveness such as summaries of student feedback, department evaluations, how you responded to student feedback – as in your own reflections and actions or planning actions.
- An outline of goals for the next 3–5 years relating to your teaching.

Material from others

- Feedback from peer review and peer support. It is becoming more and more common, indeed expected, that teaching staff will engage in peer observation and support with colleagues. This will of course only be effective if it is taken seriously and approached with professionalism.

- Feedback on course materials, assignments and other aspects of academic practice from students and colleagues.
- Student evaluation data, which is obtained during the course or at the end of the course you are teaching and from which you have considered any actions to take on the basis of student views.
- Honours or recognition such as departmental or national teaching awards.

Products of teaching/student learning

- Student learning outcomes such as grades, retention, achievement in class and on continuous assessment assignments.
- Examples of student work and the feedback given to students. If your portfolio is intended to show quality data, it must include some evidence of student achievement. However, an aspect of student achievement may be linked to how they receive feedback and the quality of that feedback. This is useful information for showing one's commitment to students.
- Student achievements in the form of presentations, conference inputs or publications on course-related work.

This is by no means an exhaustive list of material and neither is it meant to be in any way prescriptive but it is intended to give an overview of the sorts of evidence it is possible to gather, select, organise and reflect on in respect to your teaching expertise.

It is recognised that it is problematic to answer the question 'what constitutes excellence in teaching?' It all depends on the mission of the college or university context, demographics of the student bodies. 'Drivers' such as widening access, student diversity and new technologies persuade us that we need to manage our teaching differently, the question for us to answer is not 'what constitutes excellence?', the question is 'what impact does my teaching have in relation to changing the ways in which learners understand, experience or conceptualise the world around them regarding ideas, hypotheses or theories characteristic of the field of learning in which they are studying?' (Ramsden, 2003, p.8).

This is a much more challenging issue to respond to than merely claiming excellence through presenting sets of notes and PowerPoint slides and best sets of responses to evaluation questionnaires. This is the thinking behind an e-teaching portfolio initiative at one of New Zealand's research-led universities.

The teaching portfolio structure

The following case study of the e-teaching portfolio project is not unique to the university in question. It is in fact derived from the many examples of teaching portfolios available on the web, particularly from universities in Australia and the USA.

This initiative is being promoted by senior management recognising the tensions between research and teaching in a research-led university. The teaching portfolio will become the primary means of evaluating teaching. There are three aspects to the initiative:

1　To define a set of generic guidelines relating to structure which could then be contextualised according to disciplinary base and roles and responsibilities of individual academic staff members.
2　To combine the concept of developing/maintaining a teaching portfolio with enhanced use of technology – as in encouraging the development of an e-teaching portfolio.
3　Examining the professional development support and resources which would enable a scholarly, reflexive, evidence-based approach to portfolio development and which would support effective evaluation of portfolios in different contexts.

The model for this file is based on five aspects of teaching namely:

1　Roles, responsibilities, goals
2　Evaluations of teaching
3　Contributions to your institution or profession
4　Activities to improve instruction
5　Honour or recognition.

Each of these primary headings has a series of subheadings or sub-files which give guidance as to the sorts of issues which might constitute 'evidence' on current practice.

The first stage in developing the teaching portfolio may be considered to be the 'repository stage', although an implicit action in this stage is reflecting on/recording actions and activities.

Under 'Roles, responsibilities and goals', the expectation is that individuals would provide an indication of particular areas of expertise, the context of their teaching including learning hurdles in the specified discipline, and a statement describing teaching roles and responsibilities with a list of courses, student numbers, new course development, teaching styles and strategies etc.

The reflective aspect of this section of the portfolio would entail a statement on the linkage between the rationale for teaching goals, student learning activities or processes and student learning outcomes. From this information it might reasonably be expected that the individuals could draw out a statement on their teaching philosophy, goals and approaches. The intention of the guidance/guidelines given for sub-files under the main headings for the portfolios is to align reflection and enhancement of teaching.

The 'Evaluations of teaching' section includes responses to student evaluation questionnaires and reflections on these responses as well as documented evidence on peer observation exercises engaged in and undertaken, and unsolicited comments from students and peers – and self-evaluations.

The types of materials within this portfolio are therefore very similar to the previous descriptions of teaching portfolio contents. For other examples of teaching portfolio templates to suit different contexts and disciplines a simple search of the World Wide Web will reveal the range and scope of information currently available.

The e-teaching portfolio

In the example of the teaching portfolio initiative at a New Zealand University work is underway on enabling the development and maintenance of the e-teaching portfolio. While many colleges and universities are probably already working in or working towards a framework for e-teaching portfolios there are few documented examples of frameworks either in printed literature or on the web.

The issue that is clear is that staff will not be persuaded to use technology unless the e-platform is user friendly, reliable and flexible. However, assuming that this is the case, the key advantage of an e-portfolio over a paper-based folio, as with student learning e-portfolios, is that there is no limit to the means of presentation using technology. Information can be presented in a range of different formats using technology whereas a paper-based folio limits one to text-based presentation. The e-portfolio has the advantages of flexibility and portability and material can be easily manipulated for different purposes. A further advantage is of course that of modelling the use of technology for our students.

The proposed pilot project for the development of e-teaching portfolios will occur through the forum of the university's postgraduate accredited programme on teaching and learning. A cohort of staff members new to learning and teaching at tertiary level will be encouraged as part of the assessment strategy to develop and maintain an e-teaching portfolio.

This project will utilise the university's Learning Management System, as the repository for staff portfolios. This electronic learning environment (ELE) is widely used, with over 70 per cent of courses currently offering some level of e-learning support. Importantly, the ELE is integrated with other enterprise systems at the university, including the Student Management System, Peoplesoft HR, the Library Computer Systems and the teaching and learning development unit, and is therefore able to access multiple data files for the portfolio project.

Creating and maintaining the e-teaching portfolio

Creating the teaching portfolio is initially a process of collecting and categorising teaching artefacts against a recommended standard taxonomy or template (repository phase). As mentioned, physical file systems are probably best known in this context, where different folders store specific types of paper-based information (student work, representative exams, etc). Oftentimes this approach to portfolio development is hindered by inadequate records or access to historical teaching data (e.g. of students in past classes, grade distributions), and enterprise data systems rarely provide teachers access beyond current year information. Since all such artefacts are automatically stored and versioned in this university's ELE, they can be included in portfolios with no additional effort on the part of the staff member.

For this project there are two complementary interfaces for the portfolio structure. First, a 'Portfolio Space' created in the ELE for each staff member and structured with the recommended standard taxonomy template. This space will be accessible via the normal staff ELE interface. Second, this taxonomy will be automatically mirrored on the staff member's computer as a virtual directory structure, allowing normal 'drag-and-drop' skills to be used to populate the template. By surfacing the taxonomic structure in a familiar directory structure to users, the system should capitalise on the skills teaching staff already have. Figure 6.1 shows the normal staff interface in the ELE, with the addition of the taxonomy described earlier.

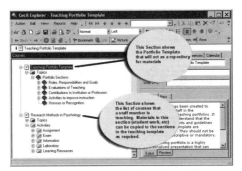

Figure 6.1 Staff interface in the electronic learning environment

Within the ELE, each file is automatically versioned and multiple instances of a filename are permitted. For instance, a single PowerPoint lecture might go through modifications over the years, and might therefore provide evidence (and reflection) of improved teaching over time. By allowing versioned copies of files, the system should provide staff with an easy and automatic means for documenting portions of their professional development.

Figure 6.2 shows the expanded portfolio taxonomy (template) that will be suggested for use by staff. This is no different from how staff often file their emails. It is designed to make it easy to file materials in an e-portfolio. A Microsoft Word template will be stored within each subcategory in the taxonomy to guide staff through both the reflection and preparation phases of their portfolio. These templates will not be prescriptive in any way, but will instead scaffold the development process for staff.

In addition, other support documents, supplementary readings and web resources will be available in appropriate sections of the template.

Professional development input on the e-teaching portfolios

The professional development input required to encourage the use of e-teaching portfolios poses a number of interesting issues. For colleges and universities there may well be contractual issues for staff that require a culture shift within the organisation. A key question may be: 'does the college or university practice what it preaches with respect to valuing the concept of a portfolio as a tool to support reflection on practice?'

Do heads of department and other line managers understand the concept of reflection, the concept of a portfolio? Do they themselves value

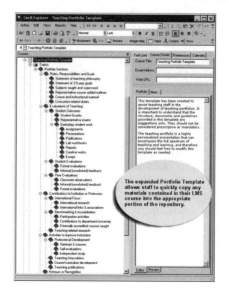

Figure 6.2 Expanded portfolio taxonomy (template)

the notion of reflection on teaching and learning? Do they recognise the importance of modelling the use of technology?

In the pilot project described here (Stefani and Diener, 2005), extensive efforts are being made to support staff in developing their e-teaching portfolio. The educational development unit facilitates a series of workshops under the following headings:

- *An introduction to Teaching Portfolios.* This seminar explains the rationale for advocating the use of teaching portfolios and institutional expectations in relation to continuation and promotion. The seminar provides opportunities to consider the typical components of teaching portfolios and the personal benefits to be gained from their preparation.

- *Writing a Teaching Philosophy.* This is a guided hands-on session in which participants have the chance to begin writing a teaching philosophy, one of the cornerstones of a teaching portfolio. Examples of teaching philosophy statements written by colleagues, particularly those who have won local and national Teaching Excellence Awards, will be made available.

- *The Role of Evidence on Teaching Portfolios.* This session provides practical advice from colleagues who have recently completed portfolios about how they collected and reported evidence about their teaching.

- *Creating and Maintaining an Electronic Teaching Portfolio.* Electronic portfolios provide an efficient way to maintain up-to-date evidence of teaching effectiveness. A template designed for a user-friendly e-portfolio structure is presented with a hands-on demonstration of how to use it to streamline the compilation and maintenance processes.
- *Portfolio-Based Assessment for Students.* This workshop examines current practice in the use of e-learning portfolios for students. Some practical examples are provided.

Obviously other colleges and universities will have their own formats for professional development. This outline of a workshop series is provided as an example of the sort of workshops one university provides based on requests from academic staff embarking on teaching portfolios and heads of departments keen to support their staff in developing e-teaching portfolios.

When sufficient numbers of staff are seen to be successfully developing and maintaining an e-teaching portfolio, it is likely that it will make it easier to encourage students to take their e-learning portfolio more seriously.

Producing a point-in-time teaching portfolio

A key component of the portfolio strategy being presented in this case study is the development of tools that allow teaching staff to easily assemble materials in a variety of ways. Central to that strategy is the ability to draw upon the materials in the e-repository as needed, and to incorporate them into templates that meet specific reporting requirements. For this reason, it is very important to the success of the project that the repository be capable of maintaining multiple versions of documents, and of maintaining metadata about those versions for selection into specific report templates.

If a staff member modifies their statement of teaching philosophy five times in as many years, each of those files will be stored by the database under a unique identifier. The name of the file (e.g. MyPhilosophy.doc) need not change, and can therefore be automatically included in templates. When generating a point-in-time portfolio the staff member simply needs to enter a date, select a template, and the most time-relevant MyPhilosophy.doc would be included in the production portfolio.

This ability will be particularly important when producing an accurate 'snapshot' view of the portfolio that reflects both the abilities and practices of the staff member and demonstrates personal reflection and improvement over time (Stefani and Diener, 2005).

The benefit of an e-teaching portfolio

As with encouraging students to develop and maintain an e-portfolio, it is proving necessary to convince staff of the benefits to them of having an e-teaching portfolio. If we are constantly highlighting the issues of reflection and lifelong learning to our students, it seems slightly hypocritical for staff not to be practising what they preach. It seems that many of the issues we need to consider for the implementation of study e-portfolios are equally applicable to e-teaching portfolios, for example purpose, framework, IT skills and assessment – albeit 'assessment' of teaching portfolios may have a slightly different meaning for staff than for students. Nevertheless, the e-teaching portfolio is essentially a tool for staff to reflect on their current and ongoing practice and it is going to be used to determine, at least in part, the career progression of the owner/author. Given the parallels between student and staff e-portfolios, it would be wonderful if staff were to lead the way for their students!

Online resources

Developing a teaching portfolio

Ohio State University. A practical and self-reflective guide. Extensive & detailed site with multiple pages covering the many different aspects of portfolio content. Available online at: <http://ftad.osu.edu/portfolio/index.html>, <http://ftad.osu.edu/portfolio/index.html#parts>, <http://ftad.osu.edu/portfolio/TableOfContents.html>.

Preparing and presenting a teaching portfolio 2005

National Tertiary Education Union – Australia's union for tertiary education staff. Comprehensive, well laid-out 36-page pdf handbook synthesising most of the best sources. For examples: page 9: table of contents and page 31–35: materials for inclusion. Available online at: <http://www.nteu. org.au/publications/other/teachingportfolio>.

Teaching portfolios

University of Texas at El Paso: Center for Effective Teaching and Learning. Tools for developing and assessing a faculty teaching portfolio – both as a formative tool and as a summative evaluation of scholarly work. Available online at: <http://sunconference.utep.edu/CETaL/resources/portfolios/>.

Teaching portfolio guidelines

Institute of Media Technology & Engineering Science at Aarlborg University, Copenhagen. From the 'University Pedagogy' Staff Development Course, available online at: <http://www.puc.aau.dk/copenhagen2006/Portfolio_guide_2006.pdf>, includes *a functional portfolio template* that can be saved in Microsoft Word. Available online at: <http://www.puc.aau.dk/copenhagen2006/Portfolio_template_2006_cph.doc>.

Compiling your teaching portfolio

Griffith University – Griffith Institute of Higher Education. Click on Illustrative Portfolios for contrasting examples appropriate to career progress. Available online at: <http://www.griffith.edu.au//centre/gihe/teachinglearning/portfolios/>.

The teaching portfolios site

University of Saskatchewan. Available online at: <http://www.usask.ca/gmcte/portfolios/parts.php> and <http://www. usask.ca/gmcte/portfolios/whatis.php>.

Teaching performance expectations (TPEs)

California State University, Northridge/Michael D. Eisner School of Education. As an organizing principle for a portfolio:13 TPEs divided between 6 major domains. Available online at: <http://www.csun.edu/~sch_educ /sed/ptp/>.

Chapter 7

E-portfolios and inclusive learning

Will e-portfolios, and e-learning more broadly, offer advantages to every student? With a general move within higher and further education to widen participation, students are now more diverse than ever before. We can no longer assume that students will be broadly similar in background, financial status, educational qualifications, culture or physical capability. Perhaps that was never a wise assumption, but it was certainly one which has underpinned the Fordist 'production' model of education where one undifferentiated educational 'product' was assumed to meet every student's needs within a particular course.

With respect to the internet and education there are some other assumptions being made. One such is that everyone is operating on a level playing field with equal access to the internet and information communication technologies in general. The progressive expansion of tertiary education to serve the majority rather than the minority has occurred alongside the drive to promote lifelong learning as an accepted cultural concept. These changes have occurred almost at the same time as the expansion in use of technology and its use in education, driving educators to take seriously the issue of equity in terms of access to and use of educational technology.

While many students entering into further or higher education have grown up with technologies such as video games, mobile phones, microcomputers and the internet, it is wrong to assume this means they are computer-savvy when it comes to using technology to support their learning. It is a mistake to assume that all students have had equal access to all of the available technologies. The onus placed on educators by recent legislation (e.g. the UK's Disability Discrimination Act, Part 4) is now very much on ensuring that where technology is used, no student should be unreasonably disadvantaged. While it is not always possible to offer every student the same level of advantage or support, each student should have sufficient access to, and ability to use, the technologies on which the course depends. From what has already been said about use of e-portfolios, these could introduce a technological tool which is central to the student's study, assessment and job search. It could even be a technology which is used throughout the student's educational career and beyond into their continuing professional development.

There is currently little published research relating to e-portfolios and access to education and technology. Nevertheless in many institutions there is serious interest in making the e-portfolio a learning tool for all at all stages and levels of learning. Future research will help to inform those implementations, and we will doubtless learn from them. However, there is a clear current need to consider the implications for e-portfolio implementation of differing levels of accessibility to technology. This chapter examines some of the issues relating to accessibility and inclusivity which are present in e-learning environments. These should help us to understand the issues for e-portfolios operated within those environments.

How inclusive is the internet?

One of the reasons why e-learning is starting to take off in colleges and universities is that computers and the internet are now widely accepted as part of the established educational scene. This follows two decades of development in technology use at home and in school. We can now expect the majority of staff and students within universities and colleges to have some level of computer literacy. Computer use and internet access are now spreading out to include children and older adults as well as those in employment who now use computers as part of their job. But while it is true that access to technology is now far less problematic than it once was, how good is it within your own institution? How relevant is students' prior use of computing and the internet to their current studies?

Very experienced internet users in a non-formal setting will not necessarily be familiar with the restrictions and etiquette that apply when using computers in education. For staff the problem is even more stark. Many will have started their teaching careers before personal computing arrived. They will have engaged with the technology as 'digital immigrants' but be expected to teach 'digital natives' (Prensky, 2001). It is also wrong to assume that all staff and students will have had equal access to all of the available technologies. Part-time teaching staff may be particularly disadvantaged by this assumption and in many institutions these make up the majority of the teaching workforce.

One of the big impacts of the internet is the extent to which it brings into the student's study resources which are not quality controlled in the same way as institutionally produced resources. When we ask students to conduct online research we are often exposing them to extensive and undifferentiated resources across the internet. Some of these may be culturally and politically offensive, others will be inaccessible to students with disability. Even when the educator links to specific resources on external sites there is no guarantee that these sites will not alter in appearance, content or functionality without the teacher being aware of this. There can be no guarantee that the internet is inclusive, although the size of the resource that it offers will generally allow students to choose alternatives. Use of quality-controlled services such as educational repositories (Jorum in the UK (http://www.jorum.ac.uk) and MERLOT in Canada (http://www.merlot.org)), will help provide greater stability. Specialist repositories such as Scottish Learning Exchange, a repository set up by the Scottish Institute for Excellence in Social Work Education (SIESWE) for social work students, set out to make all their content accessible, but such resources are, as yet, rare. The use of metadata to describe resources may in the future help disabled students to more easily identify resources which will be accessible to them, but many resources lack this level of description.

Social inclusion, learning and technology

Combating social exclusion is generally seen as an issue for the state, as it is dependent on government policies and commitment. Ideally it requires an integrated approach to tackle personal and social issues as well as structural issues. Many educational initiatives are seen as one aspect of an integrated approach and will in turn have their own local policies and practices relating to inclusion.

At the start of the new millennium, the Scottish Parliament stated that one of its priorities would be the development of a 'Digital Scotland'. Task groups were set up to look at infrastructure, education, the economy and lifelong learning. The idea was that everyone would be able to engage in this 'digital world' and the information age and that steps would be taken to prevent a digital divide and the creation of 'information rich' and 'information poor' communities. This project heralded the opening of learning centres in libraries and community centres across Scotland in an attempt to provide internet access for all. Many projects of this nature across Europe, in Australia and the United States have reported success in widening access to educational and learning opportunities. Such initiatives do, however, make it obvious that simply providing the technology is not enough. Also it is not sufficient to provide training in using specific hardware and software. Sustained use requires a focus on learning through the development of information literacy skills and information technology skills (Law, 2000). Recognising this will affect our assumptions about e-portfolio implementation. For example, it will not be sufficient to provide the hardware and software. Neither will it be enough to provide specific training in the use of the chosen e-portfolio system. The students and staff involved will require a much broader range of information literacy skills if they are to make real use of the technology, and in particular its flexibility and connectedness. As within these much broader social inclusion projects, it may be necessary within some institutions to provide hand-holding and one-to-one support tailored to particular students.

The spur to the 'Digital Scotland' initiative was to provide a positive and equable experience of using computers and the internet. Although access from home will generally be more flexible than use of central study centres and libraries we need to recognise that this is not always so. Students' access to a computer at home may be shared with others and the technology may not be very up to date (earlier or non-standard versions of software, browsers etc.). Time online may be limited by demand within the family and could also be compromised by a slow internet connection. If the student is unable to speak or fluently understand the language in which documentation is written they may need extra support and specific training. Even with good access to the best technology some students will have relatively little time for their studies (because of work, family or other commitments). Some will be studying in less than ideal conditions, for example while caring for young children in the same room.

The above points raise issues that broaden out the concept of inclusivity. For example, will not having access to technology or not having the skills or time to develop lavish multimedia e-portfolios mean that the marks of some students will suffer? Will their chances of employment be affected?

Although it is still very early to judge what the impact of e-learning may be on higher education in general, we can already see an impact on some sectors. Distance and open learning, which have often had a history of supporting social inclusion, have moved forward faster with e-learning than campus-based institutions. We could expect e-portfolios to also be relevant to part-time and distance modes of education, given the mobility of these students. For example 80 per cent of the students enrolled in courses at Athabasca University are registered for programmes elsewhere. These students are using Canada's 'open university' to find more flexible course options or accelerate their progress. As developments in the e-Bologna process continue it will become more common for students to move country, as well as institution, in order to complete their programme of study. We already have many overseas students moving countries in order to study and then returning home to work afterwards. This suggests that e-portfolios should be capable of operating across national boundaries.

Another area in which e-learning has been very influential already is in supporting and teaching students with disability. Students with disability already often rely upon personal use of assistive technologies. A student may be using an audio recorder rather than taking notes of the lecture. Another may be using voice recognition to transcribe spoken notes or assignments. Many students use photocopiers to enlarge print on handouts and in textbook. Some copy class resources onto coloured paper to help with sight problems or dyslexia. Other students may be using computer settings to increase font or change background colour.

The use of technology in teaching and learning should offer great opportunities for learning and curriculum designers to enhance the accessibility of the student learning experience. However that potential has not always been fully realised, and some commentators (Seymour and Lupton, 2004) suggest that the computer and associated technologies may actually be instruments of further alienation of people with disabilities because of our tendency to construct educational environments for the able-bodied. There may be an inherent tension here with the desire to create media-rich e-learning resources to enhance the student learning experience. This can result in the use of technologies such as Macromedia Flash animations, which may not be accessible to all students.

Whatever the learning context, it is becoming recognised that in designing learning tasks, issues of inclusion and accessibility for students with disabilities must be taken into consideration. In designing the learning environment to be more inclusive for students with disability, we also make it more usable by all students (Hammond and Stefani, 2001). For example, while students with cognitive disabilities benefit from graphics and illustrations as well as from properly organised content with heading lists and 'visual access to the navigation' (Teachability Project 2000), we can recognise that these would benefit *all* students. The remainder of this chapter focuses on the issues of accessibility and e-learning which we might expect to impact on e-portfolio implementation and use.

Understanding disability in relation to technology

The expectations of HE in relation to developing an inclusive learning environment in the UK are outlined in the QAA Code of Practice for Students with Disabilities (1999). Many of the issues relating to accessibility of FE/HE environments for students with disabilities are now well documented (e.g. Oliver, 1996; Wiles, 2002; TechDis). The major transition that has occurred is from the medical model that viewed disability as a 'personal' problem to a social model of disability that sees the response to disability as a 'societal' problem. This shift in thinking reflects a view that 'disability' is not an attribute of an individual but is created by the environment in which people with disabilities or impairments are operating. Thus a disability is defined as any restriction or lack of ability to perform an activity in a manner considered normal for people. This puts the onus on the institution to avoid being 'disabling'.

Although the implementation of specific legislation (e.g. the Disability Discrimination Act, in the UK) has helped, there are still plenty of disablist practices in society at large. In educational establishments these may manifest themselves as poor physical access, inflexible timetables, inhospitable environments and legislative infringements (Seymour and Lupton, 2004). For some students attending classes on campus would be impossible or difficult because their mobility is very severely impaired or they suffer from fatigue or other difficulties. Some prospective students will suffer from mental health problems such as depression or mental illness and these could affect their ability to attend college or class on a regular basis. The use of technology in teaching and learning allows many students in this position to remain in contact with teachers and tutors while off campus. We can see that e-portfolios could be an advantage for students who need to maintain a record of their learning over an interrupted programme of study, perhaps spanning several years and several institutions. But these advantages will only be realised if designers and facilitators of e-portfolios have an awareness of inclusivity and accessibility issues.

Not all learners will have visible or obvious disabilities. Not all disabled students will necessarily declare difficulties or disabilities before they start the course. They may not have anticipated that their disability would be a problem. We need to remember that the teacher or tutor is unlikely to be conveniently to hand at all times that the student (disabled or not) is using the e-portfolio. If the technology is not user-friendly for *all* students – not just disabled students – the use of a developmental or reflective portfolio is fundamentally affected. The development of an e-portfolio is highly personal and specific, and should be guided by the student's preferences rather than constrained by the technology. The e-portfolio cannot serve its intended purpose if the student requires a high level of support every time they need to access, add to or modify *their* e-portfolio. In this sense accessible implementation is more challenging than merely providing accessible resources with which the student does not directly interact. The e-portfolio is both a set of resources *and* a set of tools.

You should also remember that staff as well as students may be disabled. The systems that are used for viewing, commenting on and marking the student e-portfolio will also need to be accessible. You will need to consider, and ask your students to consider, how showcase e-portfolios could be made accessible to disabled employers. For example it would be good practice to format content so that magnification software can be used. Students should at least understand enough to avoid small fixed-size fonts, unusual typefaces or other inaccessible approaches.

E-learning design for accessibility

Paul Bohman of WebAIM writes,

> Where can you find Web-based multimedia content that has been fully captioned for the deaf? What if the Internet content is only accessible by using a mouse? And what if web developers use all graphics instead of text. If screen readers can only read text how would they read the graphics to people who are blind? When these types of questions are posed, it becomes clear that there are a few potential glitches in the accessibility of the Internet to people with disabilities. The Internet has the potential to revolutionize disability access to information but without due care and attention to inclusive practice it is just as possible to place further obstacles along the way that diminish that potential and which leave people with disabilities just as discouraged and dependent on others as before.
>
> (Bohman, 2003)

There are many excellent accessibility advisors and services geared to the needs of higher and further education. It is likely that you have experts within your own institution advising course developers. You will need to liaise with them to achieve an accessible e-portfolio implementation in your own context. The level of accessibility that Bohman looks for is not achieved by accident. At the end of this chapter we have recommended some excellent sources of information to guide you.

Difference in disability

The major categories of disability include:

- *Visual* – blindness, low vision, colour blindness.
- *Hearing* – deafness, impairment.
- *Motor* – inability to use a mouse, slow response time, limited fine motor control.
- *Cognitive* – learning disabilities, distractability, inability to remember or focus on large amounts of information.

However, each type of disability within these categories will bring its own challenges and solutions. Some students will use specific technologies – assistive technologies – to help them. Others may use able-bodied helpers.

Some students may have multiple disabilities. A student with the same disability as another may not require or choose the same type of assistance. This could be because of financial or technological constraints, familiarity and preferences, or simply because the student has no knowledge of the alternatives. The aids that a student may use in the classroom could be different from those they use at home, where they may have less portable but more effective systems set up.

Below we have suggested some of the questions that you might wish to consider when planning an e-portfolio implementation that is suitable for dyslexic students. This example looks at the choices and issues in some detail. For other disabilities the choices and issues may be quite different.

The number of students with disability entering further and higher education is growing, but dyslexia is probably the fastest growing group. In the UK, in 2002, 16,490 first year undergraduates identified themselves as dyslexic compared to just 2,360 in 1994, a sevenfold increase in eight years (HESA). Many students will not have realised that they had dyslexia until they progressed to tertiary education. It is also not a visible condition, so if students do not inform the institution that they are dyslexic then their teacher may not know. Dyslexia impacts on:

- *Visual processing abilities* – which can lead to slow visual object recognition, problems with visual concentration and over-sensitivity to light.
- *Phonological decoding, analysis and processing* – relating to the ability to recognise, produce and sequence letter sounds leading to poor written expression.
- *Reading and comprehension* – there are particular issues for students assessed as dyslexic.

- *Auditory processing* – this can be problematic for many students particularly in terms of attention span.
- *Memory recall* – dyslexia impacts on the short term and working memory.
- *Structure and sequencing of text* – students can get lost in a hyper-text structure so it is particularly important that the architecture of websites is user-friendly and well thought out for ease of navigation.

Providing information in text form rather than in the form of speech would appear to disadvantage dyslexics if we understand this condition as simply one of 'word-blindness'. However, as the above list shows, a text record could be helpful to dyslexic students who need to review the instructions several times to make sure that they have remembered or correctly inter-preted them. Planning and organisation of websites and the materials being presented are important for all students. For dyslexic students, key information, instructions and tasks should be towards the top of a page with introductory text explaining the page/section content and expecta-tions of the students. Language should be simple and unambiguous.

TechDis, part of the UK's Higher Education Academy, aims to enhance provision for students and staff with disabilities in higher, fur-ther and specialist and community education through the use of technology. They provide advice on dyslexia. In Table 7.1 we have adapted some of this general advice to show how meeting the needs of dsylexics could impact on e-portfolio design.

Many of the recent changes in colleges and universities which relate to students with disabilities have come about through legislation or other external drivers. At a time when student retention is a key operational objective, teaching and support staff can feel under pressure to reconcile two conflicting priorities (retention and widening participation). There may also be legitimate staff concerns about pressure on resources. It is even possible that some staff are relatively ignorant about current research into certain disabilities. For example they may be sceptical about the effects of conditions such as dyslexia, attention deficit disorder or ME.

Some institutions have tried to update views on disability and inclu-sion through institutional initiatives. In the UK Open University all staff were required in 2005 to undertake Diversity Training and pass an assessment which tested their knowledge of discrimination and diversity issues. In Australia the Creating Accessible Teaching and Support (CATS) project, funded by the Australian Universities Teaching Committee, produced a series of booklets relating to inclusive practice for staff and students with disabilities. The materials are available on the

Table 7.1 E-portfolio design considerations relating to dyslexic students

Helpful design approaches	Why this helps dyslexic students and staff	How this may impact on e-portfolio implementation
Providing appropriate (and ideally variable) contrast in the colours of text and background	Dark text on pale background is generally easier to read. Some high contrasts can be difficult to read e.g. black on white.	If a decision is made to 'brand' e-portfolios, following a common institutional design, it will be important to allow individual settings by users. These should 'persist' so that on login a user will see the settings they prefer on any of the machines that they use.
Sequential presentation of content	This will be helpful for all students but is particularly useful for slower readers. Research shows that all readers access text at a slower rate on a computer and this should be taken into consideration when putting information on the web.	It is worth considering keeping the design of the e-portfolio similar in lay-out to other webpages that the student may already be familiar with. The student will then know where to find information that they have previously reviewed.
Design webpages to reduce burden on users spatial visualisation and visual motor coordination	The format of printed text does not translate accessibly to the web. One design approach is to reduce overall information density to less than 50% of the screen area.	Shorter webpages require less scrolling and may appear less intimidating. However there must be good navigation to allow the user to find their way between web pages.
Font size is important for visual accessibility of text	Fonts should be easy to read, have clear definable letter shapes and have clear spacing between letter combinations.Reader friendly fonts include Verdana, Georgia, Tahoma and Trebuchet MS.	All students should be encouraged to use read able, accessible fonts, for their e-portfolio submissions. This will assist any dyslexic readers of their material (fellow students, staff, potential employers).

Helpful design approaches	*Why this helps dyslexic students and staff*	*How this may impact on e-portfolio implementation*
Text should be left justified	This is a good 'default'. Right-aligned text is difficult to read and so is most justified text. Again the ideal is for users to have some control over presentation.	Again this is good design practice for all e-portfolio authors.
Websites should be designed so that they offer a variety and cues for readers	A good webpage design can be easily understood without reading or scanning large amounts of text. It may use headings, large type, bold text, highlighted text, bullet points, icons, graphics and tables to make the page more visually memorable.	If the system is being used across several courses and departments it will be important to achieve some uniformity in the design approach so that students do not have to relearn the clues each time. For example, standard icons are helpful visual clues for dyslexics, but must be used consistently.
Provide a map as a navigational overview	A clear site map will provide a visual overview to which the student can return and from which they can 'find' the areas that they need.	Navigational devices such as 'breadcrumb trails' which show the progress through the site will help all users. For the dyslexic they can act as a memory aid of what happens next in the e-portfoilio sequence.
Key information should be made more prominent	Key information such as learning outcomes, assessment criteria and online expectations should be made obvious. It should be possible to return to review this information easily from any webpage.	With an e-portfolio system which students will be using year-on-year it may be worth identifying what is new in the key information so that students are not expected to read standard information every year. Dyslexic students may find it difficult to spot what is different this year.

Helpful design approaches	Why this helps dyslexic students and staff	How this may impact on e-portfolio implement
Allow a variety of text input devices and file formats	Dyslexic students may wish to dictate entries using voice recognition rather than writing notes using a keyboard. They may wish to use software such as Wordshark to help them to spell words correctly. Being able to cut and paste from specialist programmes can be helpful. Web designs which require direct input of text with no built-in spellchecker are not helpful.	In considering what content can be used within an e-portfolio you may wish to support mind-mapping (which some dyslexics find helpful) and a variety of audio and video file formats. Dyslexic e-portfolio owners may be more comfortable providing reflections as audio entries rather than as text. This may however have implications for assessment.

CATS website (http://www.adcet.edu.au/cats). These publications include supporting students with visual impairments, hearing impairments and mental health conditions.

In one of the CATS case studies, relating to ensuring access to technologically based information sources such as the library catalogue, CD-ROMs and the internet, a student remarks

> I know it's important to go to tutorials and take part in discussion, but sometimes it's just so stressful that I'd rather fail than turn up. My tutor has arranged for me to take part in online discussions so that I still have the interaction with others in my class but in an environment I find less threatening. She also makes sure that I receive all feedback on my work in writing. This means that I can read it in my own time and really understand what the tutor is trying to tell me.
>
> (Third Year Arts student)

We can hope that in the future there will be many more examples of using technology to enable, rather than disable students. An e-portfolio medium for learning could be ideally suited to the Arts student quoted above. But we need to be mindful of the impact on students with different impairments. A student with a visual impairment could benefit from the audio and video input opportunities, but could find many online environments difficult to navigate.

We are not suggesting that the solution to making websites accessible is to make them less attractive and exciting. This, as Steyaert (2005) points out, is mythology arising from an uncreative response to accessibility which emphasises non-graphic, text-only designs. As we have seen, graphics and stylistic variety are important if a website is to be optimally accessible to students with some types of disability, for example dyslexia. Providing flexibility to users of software or online applications means allowing users to change colour, font size, screen layout according to their needs and preferences. It should allow for the display of the content in a number of different ways. For example with audio turned off, with screen-readable text to supplement or replace graphics, with captioning of digital video, with descriptions to accompany flash animations. This is not a dull prospect, rather it provides exciting challenges to use all the tools at our disposal to make e-learning attractive to all.

It is unlikely that you will design an accessible and usable e-portfolio system if you do not start with that objective clearly in mind. A second myth Steyaert (2005) suggests that we 'debunk', is that accessibility features can be bolted on at the end, as an afterthought. This is equivalent to saying that in designing, developing and delivering the curriculum in a traditional classroom based mode we can take 'special needs' considerations at a later stage, bolt them on and continue to discriminate against students by setting them up as a 'special needs group' rather than work towards designing an inclusive curriculum in the first place.

Bohman (2003) points out that it is no more problematic to create accessible websites than it is to create inaccessible ones. The real issue for web developers is an awareness of the issues associated with accessibility. Once developers understand the concepts, implementing them becomes simply part of their role, part of the application of their skills. It need not add time or cost on to the process of developing the sites.

Providing all students with choice and flexibility will lead to a richer learning experience for all. As Shakespeare (2005), a well-known spokesperson for disability rights, suggests, 'We need to be open to the differences that differences make'. This requires openness to diversity and difference, to flexibility and customisation. In effect a more specifically student-centred approach to teaching. It also reminds us that inclusiveness is an opportunity, and a necessity, as well as an obligation.

Our aim should be to create an e-portfolio system that is as accessible as possible for as many learners as possible.

Useful resources for e-learning and accessibility

Bohman, P. (2003) *Introduction to Web Accessibility,* WebAIM: Web Accessibility in Mind pp. 1–6. Available at: <http://www.webaim.org/ info> (Accessed 20 February 2006).

Law, D. (2000) 'Information policy for a new millennium', *Library Review* 49(7): 322–330.

Seymour, W. and Lupton, D. (2004) 'Holding the line online: exploring wired relationships for people with disabilities'. *Disability and Society* 19(4): 291–305.

Steyaert, J. (2005) 'Web-based Higher Education, the inclusion/exclusion Paradox', *Journal of Technology in Human Services* 23(1): 67–78.

TechDis (2004) 'Accessibility do's and don'ts for beginners'. Available at: <http://www.techdis.ac.uk/index.php?p=1_20040511081154_20042411011 107> (Accessed 20 February 2006).

TechDis (2003) 'A dyslexic perspective on e-content accessibility' (Rainger, P.F.). Available at: <http://www.techdis.ac.uk/sevenpapers/> (Accessed 10 February 2006).

EDNER (2002) *Formative Evaluation of the Distributed National Electronic Resource Project 2002.* Web Accessibility Issues for Higher and Further Education. Issue Paper 6. Available at: <http://www.cerlim.ac.uk/edner/ip/ip 06.rtf>.

Hopkins, L. (ed.) (2000) *Library Services for Visually Impaired People: A Manual of Best Practice.* Resource: the Council for Museums, Archives and Libraries. Library and Information Commission Research Report 7b. STV/LIC Programme Report 10.

Singleton, C. (1999*) The Report of the National Working Party on Dyslexia in Higher Education.* National Working Party on Dyslexia in Higher Education Hull: University of Hull (ISBN 1 898862 99 0).

Taite, T. (2000) *General Strategies for Revising and Editing on Computers.* Literacy Education Online (LEO). Available online at: <http//leo.stcloud-state.edu/acadwrite/computerediting.html> (Accessed 20 February 2006).

World Wide Web Consortium. Available at: http://www.w3.org/> (Accessed 27 February 2006).

W3C Web Accessibility Initiative (last update September 2005). Available at: <http://www/w3.org/WAI/> (Accessed 27 February 2006).

Britain, S. and Liber, O. (1999) *A Framework for Pedagogical Evaluation of Virtual Learning Environments.* JTAP, JISC Technology Applications. Available at: <http://www.jisc.ac.uk/uploaded_documents/jtap-041.doc> (Accessed 10 February 2006).

Ingraham, B. and Bradburn, E. (2003) *Set Back and Relax: A Guide to Producing Readable, Accessible Onscreen Text.* Available at: <http://readabil-ity.tees.ac.uk> (Accessed 10 February 2006).

e-Learning Centre: information and services. Available at: <http://www.e-learn-ingcentre.co.uk/eclipse/Resources/accessible.htm> (Accessed 1 February 2006).

Skills for Access: *The Comprehensive Guide to Creating Accessible Multimedia for e-Learning.* Available at: <http://www.skillsforaccess.org.uk> (Accessed 01 February 2006).

CATS – Creating Accessible Teaching and Support (for students with disabilities). Available online at: <http://www.adcet.edu.au/cats>

Chapter 8

Software solutions for a complex concept

In previous chapters, the issue of what tools to use for successful e-portfolio implementation has been mentioned in overall contexts. The aim of this chapter is to focus specifically on current thinking relating to e-portfolio systems. The IMS e-portfolio specification suggests that the types of information an e-portfolio can contain are:

- about digital and non-digital works created or part-created by the subject
- about the subject of the e-portfolio
- about activities in which the subject has participated, is participating, or plans to participate
- about the competencies (skills, etc.) of the subject
- about the achievements of the subject, whether or not certificated
- about the subject's preferences
- about the subject's goals and plans
- about the subject's interests and values
- any notes, reflections or assessments relevant to any other part
- the results of any test or examination of the subject
- contextual information to help the interpretation of any results
- the relationships between the other parts of the information (see elsewhere for discussion)
- about the creation and ownership of the parts of the e-portfolio.

It goes on to provide six categories of e-portfolio:

1   Assessment – used to demonstrate achievement against some criteria
2   Presentation – used to evidence learning in a persuasive way, often related to professional qualifications

3   Learning – used to document, guide and advance learning over time
4   Personal development – related to professional development and employment
5   Multiple-owner – allows more than one person to participate in development of content
6   Working – combines previous types, with one or more e-portfolios and also a wider archive.

Most institutions would, in fact, want the functionality of all six of these categories. However, most institutions do not adopt e-portfolios for all students and all staff all at once. Rather, the initiative is usually led by one or two early adopters for use on one course or programme. This makes it difficult for an institution to determine which product will best meet its needs.

Types of e-portfolio software

At this point in the development of e-portfolio software, there are four categories of systems in use and as might be expected, there are pros and cons to adopting any one of them:

Commercial software

Just as with ELEs, many institutions choose simply to purchase a commercial system from a recognised vendor and take on board the customary licensing and support fees.

Pros:

- No direct software development costs
- Technical support is handled by the vendor
- There are a number of e-portfolio software systems to choose from
- A content management system (CMS) may have a built in e-portfolio solution. This obviously keeps the e-portfolio tool within an integrated environment rather than licensing two different applications.

Cons:

- Licenses must adapt to the vendor's pricing structure
- Customer service and technical support may be poor
- Requests for adaptations may be expensive and take too long.

Proprietary systems (often designed by universities)

Many universities have the capacity and interest to design their own software. Or they may have legacy systems that they want to integrate with the e-portfolio e.g. online submission of assignments and recording of grades and degrees.

Pros:

• The institution develops exactly what it wants
• No software licensing fees are involved
• The institution owns the intellectual property.

Cons:

• Hardware and software development costs can be prohibitive
• The system may require too much time and energy to build
• High levels of software development and technical expertise are required to build and maintain the system
• The institution may not be able to retain expert staff long enough to sustain and scale the system.

Open source e-portfolio software

This approach is steadily gaining adherents, as the software develops. The Open Source Portfolio Initiative (OSPI) is a collaborative effort to create a more robust electronic portfolio application through the combined efforts of the open source community.

Pros:

• There is no charge for open source software
• Members of OSPI participate in the development of the software
• OSPI is designed to work with the Sakai Project – a community-source software development effort to build a 'collaboration and learning environment' for higher education.

Cons:

• There are costs associated with technical support and maintenance
• There is the possibility of an open source initiative dying out and the

community disbanding which poses risks related to replacement costs

• Software development and upgrades may not keep pace with needs.

The Open Source Portfolio Initiative (http://www.osportfolio.org/) is a community of individuals and organisations collaborating to develop the leading non-proprietary, open source electronic portfolio software. Several universities particularly in the United States are using open source software to 'build' their portfolio system. The OSPI website gives detailed information on current developments in OSPI and also provides a number of case studies of universities using OSPI. For colleges or universities considering implementing an e-portfolio approach to teaching and learning, these case studies provide helpful information on: why the institution adopted OSP; the background and context of their e-portfolio initiative; the goals of the portfolio initiative and the challenges and issues faced by the institution in setting up an e-portfolio initiative.

Open source common tools

Lorenzo and Ittelson (2005) document a fourth basic approach to e-portfolio systems: the use of open source publicly available software, not designed especially for e-portfolios, but adaptable by creative users. For example, an institution might decide to use HTML editors such as Microsoft Front Page or Macromedia Dreamweaver to support the development of e-portfolios.

Pros:

• More creative e-portfolios are possible – users are not locked into a predefined style with predefined fields to fill
• Allows e-portfolio creators to design and enter artefacts in any way they please
• Software costs are very low.

Cons:

• Requires students to have web-authoring skills such as an understanding of HTML rather than being guided by a template driven approach which enables web pages to be created (from Lorenzo and Ittelson 2005).

A discussion of these four options forms the body of this chapter.

Commercial systems

There are a range of commercial systems available; the one chosen to discuss here is ePortaro. The folio by ePortaro is described as the leading enterprise-level electronic portfolio software system; ePortaro say of their software that it has the following characteristics:

- User-centred security controls to determine which items are available for which users
- Portfolio data forms can capture reusable and searchable information about the user and his/her achievements
- Items can be 'certified' by the institution as authentic
- Information can be stored in a wide range of formats
- Users can create their own highly customized output layouts
- Supervisory controls can be defined to allow access to student materials and portfolios for advising and tutoring
- Built-in e-mail capability to inform outside parties of a new public portfolio
- A browser-based interface that meets ADA and internet accessibility standards
- It is developed from the ground up for the web and is highly scalable and configurable to support a wide range of users.

Current users include Glasgow Caledonian, Deakin, Stanford, Philadelphia, Vanderbilt and Drexel Universities; ePortaro is marketed by Sentient in Europe and has partnerships with Blackboard/WebCT and Questionmark. Facilities include portfolio templates, personal development logs and assessment facilities. Institutions considering ePortaro could find out more about its capabilities and capacities through dialogue with current users.

Proprietary (university-designed) software

There are many more proprietary systems in use than commercial systems at the moment. The one discussed here is that designed by Zayed University in the United Arab Emirates. It is called The Learning Outcomes ePortfolio and supports the Zayed University academic program model by providing an infrastructure designed to support an outcomes-based learning and assessment program. It provides support for students to demonstrate development in the six ZU Learning Outcomes:

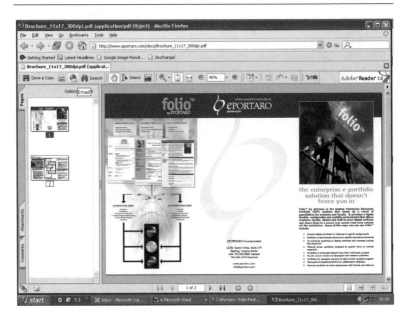

Figure 8.1 Screenshot of ePortaro software

Source: ePortaro, http://www. eportaro.com/docs/ Brochure_11x17_300 dpi.pdf

critical thinking and reasoning, information literacy and communication, information technology, global awareness, teamwork, and leadership and it supports faculty in assessing students' achievements. All students enrolled in Zayed University are required to complete a digital portfolio. This e-portfolio may include webpages, documents, PowerPoint presentations, hyperlinks, images, digital audio and/or video or any other digital media as evidence of proficiency in the learning outcomes. Reflections on students' yearly progress in each of the six learning outcome areas accompany their evidence. Faculty assessors review this material, attend the student's presentation, question the student, and submit assessments to the e-portfolio at the end of the student's third year.

Learning Outcomes e-portfolios demonstrate students' academic achievement and personal growth, integrate educational experiences, be they formal or informal, curricular or extracurricular, present examples of students' work and reflective writings that demonstrate the student's understanding and attainment of the ZU Learning Outcomes and prepare students for Capstone experiences and final assessments before graduation. Faculty are encouraged to review their students' e-portfolios in order to assist them in building knowledge and skills within specific areas. The student's Learning Outcomes e-portfolio becomes a roadmap leading them toward understanding and achieving the skills necessary to live and work in today's world and in tomorrow's changing environment.

Another proprietary piece of e-portfolio software is for the Canadian school system and was designed by the Centre for the Study of Learning and Performance at Concordia University. The software is designed for use in French and English classrooms within Canadian elementary and secondary schools. The design of the software is the result of collaboration with Quebec school board administrators, teachers, students and school board ICT consultants. The Quebec Education Programme lists the following as possible advantages of portfolios, they:

- involve students in their learning (as a tool for reflection)
- allow students to increase their ability to self-evaluate
- teach students to make choices
- encourage students to better understand themselves and focus on their strengths
- allow students to reflect on their procedures, strategies, and accomplishments so that they can improve and correct them and ultimately succeed
- promote feedback during the learning process, particularly during individual conferences
- encourage students to reflect on their strengths, needs, errors, interests, challenges, and objectives
- encourage interactive processes among students, teachers, and parents
- show student progress because it tracks performance over time; and
- are used to assess competencies developed by students.

(Wade *et al.*, 2005)

The software is continually being improved based on use in pilot schools. The aim with this project is to combine research evidence on portfolio use with practical feedback from the field, in an attempt to develop easy-to-use, powerful software designed to support the entire portfolio process. The software is available free of charge for schools who wish to partner with the developers on this project. Research involves:

- using portfolios to track an individual's process of reflecting on and analysing activities and performance
- identifying strengths and weaknesses
- using portfolios to present evidence about individual or organisational growth and development, and the differentiation and integration of knowledge

- using portfolios to support curricular innovation, connection with scholarship, and course design
- (scholarship of teaching and learning): investigating questions of teaching effectiveness in light of impact on student learning.

The project has been supported by Industry Canada, the Norshield Foundation, and by Valorisation Recherche Québec.

Open source e-portfolios

There is considerable interest in the Open Source Portfolio Initiative (OSPI) which is simply a community of individuals and organisations collaborating on the development of a non-proprietary, open source electronic portfolio software. The OSPI e-portfolio software code is freely available to anyone who would like to be a part of the project, and is currently being maintained by a consortium of universities, in collaboration with the rSmart group. Three examples of use are described here, one from the UK and two from the US.

The aim of the personal e-portfolios teaching and learning (PETAL) project in the UK is to develop an e-portfolio tool for lifelong learning based on the Open Source Portfolio Initiative. It is to provide appropriate Open Source License agreements to the software based on the OSPI licence.

The range of institutions piloting the product is very wide: Higher and Further Education, Adult Community Education and Professional Institutes. Some users, such as refugees, would only have entry-level literacy. Others would be chartered professionals.

The focus is on two related areas: accessibility and usability. This dual focus is deliberate in that software may pass the current tests on accessibility but still not be user-friendly and therefore, not accessible in reality. A critical test for PETAL is that it be adaptable to the user's skill, confidence and reading level/ability, among other things.

One of the hopes for the pilots is that through e-portfolios, many learners can overcome their sense of failure experienced in previous education activities. E-portfolios encourage learners to list their successes, no matter how informally acquired. Further details can be found online at http://www.jiscmail.ac.uk/lists/myWorld.html.

Two American examples are from Virginia Tech and Portland State University who choose OSP because of the capacity for in-house customisation according to institutional goals. In the case of Portland State University, the goals are:

- to expand the practice of e-portfolios throughout all four years of their university studies general education programme
- to integrate e-portfolio practices with general teaching and learning activities in the context of an enterprise learning management system
- to incorporate e-portfolio use into departments and majors across campus
- to enhance faculty use of e-portfolios for promotion, tenure and annual performance review
- to use OSP for institutional portfolio and aggregating data across campus
- to utilize OSP to showcase student and faculty work for external audiences.

This list of uses in Portland State University demonstrates the flexibility of OSP for student, staff and institutional e-portfolios.

In a case study of this example, written by Wende Morgaine and Nate Angell (2006), a number of useful pointers about the implementation of OSP are raised. Some of the recommendations are likely to be of use to all institutions considering e-portfolios irrespective of the software being used. For example, Morgaine and Angell suggest:

- starting with small pilot projects and building on success as a basis for expanding use
- allowing much more time than you initially think necessary to train staff in using the software before beginning a pilot project
- appointing an enthusiastic faculty member as opposed to someone from IT services to manage the implementation. Staff are likely to be more enthusiastic if technology is being used for pedagogical rather than technological reasons
- securing buy-in from key staff including administrative staff before the software becomes vital to mission critical operations.

Likewise, users of the VTeP system at Virginia Tech, built on the OSPI e-portfolio, have found that it is critical to ensure staff are well trained in the use of the software. Both staff and students need to be persuaded into 'folio thinking' and understand how to meaningfully incorporate e-port-folios into teaching and learning strategies. Endorsement of the e-portfolio initiative by senior management helps to build interest and adoption of the system. The second finding is that adequate technical platform support is necessary so that upscaling of the project is possible.

All of the case studies presented on the OSPI website give information on the types of servers and other software applications being used in conjunction with OSPI.

Open source common tools

Lorenzo and Ittelson (2005) describe a common tools approach to e-portfolios at St Olaf College. The web-portfolio approach at St Olaf was not driven by programme assessment, career development, certification requirements or accreditation purposes. Rather the college's decision to adopt web-portfolios was motivated entirely by considerations of pedagogy and student intellectual development.

The student e-portfolios are created by Dreamweaver and appear to consist of collections of the student's work with hyperlinks to demonstrate understanding of the relationships between different achievements. Lorenzo and Ittelson (2005) suggest that the St Olaf portfolios reveal a wide range of styles with some students displaying more skills at website building than others. This is compatible with the point raised earlier that in a common tools approach to e-portfolios, students require different skill sets. At St Olaf College some students show a high level of sophistication in displaying their learning experiences while others just load materials into folders and index them.

In a system such as this it is to be expected that some students understand and appreciate the value of the portfolio whereas others see it as an extra burden. In the system the individual student portfolios can be burned onto a CD and presented to the students at graduation. This is not dissimilar to the example highlighted in an earlier chapter from the University of Strathclyde. Portfolios such as this are not necessarily seen as an integral aspect of the institution's expectations of students, but rather of the overall teaching and learning culture.

Choosing appropriate software

The above analysis seems to indicate that there is no really dominant market leader at the moment. Many systems have been developed by universities and so are used on particular courses, but no real market penetration has occurred. Very few of the products are enterprise level solutions, and many are hosted services, which would not suit education needs for integration. This is a market at an early state, and with a particular higher education focus so, as in the early stages of ELEs, many universities are creating their own, before the market settles down. This immaturity in the market makes it difficult to determine a likely winner, and most products have shortcomings depending on individual institutions' purposes. What should not be forgotten is that today's learners are more likely to be enthusiastic about technology provided they are being asked to use it in a manner that seems relevant to them. To interest students in the first instance it may be that encouraging the use of simple blogs or wikis is an excellent starting point.

New products will come on to the market all the time. A simple web search will produce thousands of references to e-portfolios in schools, colleges and universities. The best approach for institutions now is to communicate with users of different products and determine which is the best software solution for the culture, context, goals and aspirations of the institution. It is time-consuming and resource-intensive to set up e-portfolio initiatives. There are enough examples of good practice now for new adopters to avoid expensive pitfalls or even piloting with the wrong software for the given context.

As an aid to institutions setting up portfolio projects Nuventive (2006) have produced a checklist document entitled 'Electronic Portfolio Solutions: Performance and Requirements Analysis'. This document is designed to help identify if the portfolio software solution your organisation is reviewing meets current or future requirements. It is a simple rating tool with a scale of 1 (unacceptable) to 5 (superior implementation). It is well worthwhile using this tool within a focus group or staff development context. The tool has six sections covering specifications for:

- Portfolio ownership
- Portfolio reviewers
- Institutions and portfolio administration requirements
- Assessment considerations
- Analysis and reporting
- Advanced technology.

The questions covered in this tool are comprehensive and could help decision-making when considering different software options.

Standards and specifications

There is currently much debate around the issue of the need for e-portfolio standards and specifications. On the one hand it is argued that the proliferation of e-portfolio applications requires compatible software and design standards to support lifelong learning. As Treuer and Jenson (2003) point out e-portfolios need standards in order to thrive: standards are needed to enable portability of e-portfolios across applications to allow for comparability of portfolio data across organisations and for the interoperability of applications with other systems. There is an increasing emphasis on ensuring that learners, as they transfer between different educational institutes, can transport their e-portfolios into new systems. This has led the IMS Global Learning Consortium to offer an e-portfolio specification that will provide a standard for interoperability among software systems and support for the transfer of learner products, materials and records between disparate portfolio systems that adopt it. For whole institution adoption of an e-portfolio approach to learning, it should be considered essential to understand the importance of interoperability before choosing a software system.

On the other hand heavily regulated efforts to standardise portfolios may well stifle creativity and innovation. According to Siemens (2004), in order for a tool or a technology to succeed it must be adapted at the end-user level. He believes that the field of learning objects seems currently to be hindered in development due to the proliferation of complex standards. There is an assumption that interoperability is what end-users actually need when in fact people are already sharing learning objects with peers and colleagues using simple tools such as PowerPoint presentations, notes, Word documents, graphics etc. In this way objects do not need to be repackaged to fit standards specifications. Siemens (2004) believes that e-portfolios will be successful if the excessive urge to standardise is resisted and if interoperability is built into the sharing structure using technologies such as Really Simple Syndication (RSS) and Simple Object Access Protocol (SOAP) social networking tools rather than into the content itself.

Other researchers in the field of e-portfolios believe that standards should guarantee interoperability of data and services. Treuer and Jensen (2003) believe that for educators to build e-portfolios useful to each learner regardless of age, area of residence, or institutional affiliation they will have to create a common set of standards for electronic portfolio design. They believe that this is the only way portfolios can truly become an educational passport useful in any type of educational setting as well as for professional development in any career path.

While the debate over portfolio standards will presumably continue Treuer and Jensen (2003) have given a helpful starting point for e-portfolio developers to think about regarding standards for the major functional areas of portfolios – entering, storing and sharing. Their list of standards is not incompatible with the view that an ideal portfolio system should allow:

- flexible input with each item having its own metadata and treated as a unique object
- organisation of objects or artefacts into folders
- display of items where permission is granted for intended audiences.

If these conditions are met for the e-portfolio, it should become a useful tool for learners, educators and institutions. E-portfolio standards can of course cover a wider range of issues such as document format (eg: pdf, html, tml, etc), accessibility (eg: WAI), data format (eg: learner profile), authentification (eg: certificates), access rights, etc. IMS specifications such as LIP (learning information profile) and content packaging are some of the elements that could be included in future e-portfolio standards. The most critical issue for any organisation is to make the decision on what exactly they see as the overarching purpose of the portfolio. As this chapter has shown, the options for e-portfolio software systems range from simple web tools to complex integrated commercial software, to open source solutions to in-house tailored-to-need enterprise systems.

Options reviewed

This chapter has presented four options and provided discussion and examples of them. In fact the choice is more clear-cut than it might appear:

1   If your users do not have considerable web skills, the Open Source common tools approach is probably not appropriate.
2   If your institution does not have the resources to develop a proprietary system, choose a commercial system.
3   If your institution cannot support the overhead of an Open Source e-portfolio, then choose a commercial system.
4   If your institution has not committed to a full implementation of e-portfolios, then begin with blogs and consider trying a commercial system.

Case example: Using SPIDER at Strathclyde University

The following is an extract of a personal development portfolio from the Strathclyde University system, called SPIDER. It gives a taste of the kind of instructions students receive and the options available.

Figure 8.2 The SPIDER Electronic Personal Development Portfolio

Using the Electronic Personal Development Portfolio

Your e-PDP – Electronic Personal Development Portfolio – is intended to assist you in compiling your personal development material and keeping it up to date over the 4 years of your study. It also provides a means of sharing this information with your counsellor. The e-PDP forms part of the science faculty's SPIDER virtual learning environment. So if you are registered with SPIDER you have an e-PDP. You can access your e-PDP from any computer on the campus network, or your home computer if you have one.

Logging on to SPIDER

First log on to SPIDER using Internet Explorer (or any other web browser) by opening the web page

spider.science.strath.ac.uk

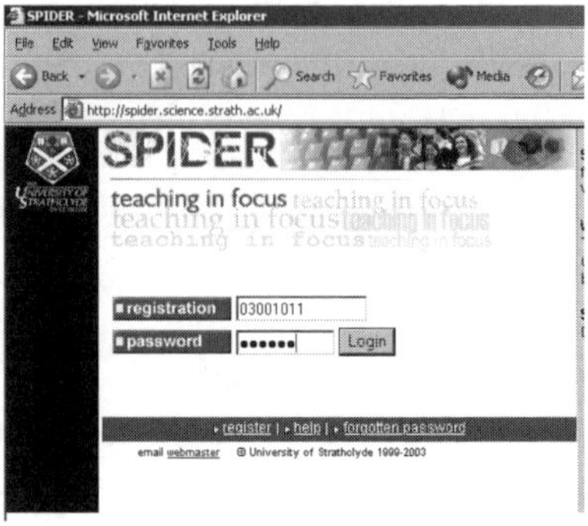

Enter your student registration number and password and click

(Note. If you have not registered with SPIDER, click the **register** link and follow the procedure to obtain a password.)

Accessing your e-PDP page

After logging in to SPIDER you are presented with your personal SPIDER home page.

Click the ![icon] button at the right side of the **My Stuff** menu to display the My Stuff options.

■ my Stuff ▲
▷ my Quiz results
▷ my Exam results
▷ my Files
▷ my Assignments
▷ my PDP
▷ myMessages
▷ Email
▷ my Groups

then click the **myPDP** option to display your e-PDP page.

The e-PDP page

Your PDP contains:

- Your personal skills profile

- Your development diary

- Your course work portfolio

- Your personal details

You can add, delete and edit any items within these categories through this page.

The personal skills profile

The aim of the personal skills profile table is to provide you with a tool to help you review your current range of personal skills and to try to identify both those that you consider to be your strengths and those that need to be worked upon. Using it can help you determine which areas you might prioritise as part of your development programme.

To view your personal skills profile, click the manage your personal skills rating option on your myPDP page.

Rating your skills

To create a new ratings profile, select the rating you think most appropriate for each skill in the New ratings column. Each skill is rated according to the following criteria:

1   I do this very well. I am consistent and successful in it.
2   I am good at this. With some practice, I can make it perfect.
3   I am getting better, but still need to work on this a bit more.
4   I am not particularly good at this – yet!

When you have completed the table, click the Save my skills button to add the ratings into the table.

The development diary

The development diary is intended to help you assess your progress in developing the range of skills needed by a graduate and to form a focus of discussion with your counsellor. In your diary, you can list the skill areas that you have identified as needing work done on them and the practical plans you have put in place to improve them.

To add a new entry to your development diary:

a) Click the add entry to diary option on your myPDP page.
b) Select the category of skill from the Title list.
c) Enter a short description of the skill that you think you need to develop into the Skill Area box.
d) Enter a short description of the steps that you plan to take to improve the identified skill in the Development Plan box.
e) Click the Add button.

Your diary entries are listed on your e-PDP page by the date when they were created and topic. You (and your counsellor) can view each entry by clicking its View button. You can edit the contents of a diary entry, by clicking its Edit button. If you want to delete the entry completely, click the Delete button.

Course Work

The course work area of your e-PDP is designed to hold a list of key documents which provide examples of your course work.

Adding documents

To add a document to your record:

a) Select the Manage my Coursework link on your my PDP page.

b) Click the Browse button and select the document to be added to your record.

c) Enter the title by which the document will be listed in the Link name box.

d) If you want to add some extra information, enter it into the Extra Info box.

e) If you want to make the document visible to your counsellor, select the Public option from the Status list. If you want it only to be accessible by yourself, select Private. (Note that you can return and change the Public/Private setting of a document whenever you wish.)

f) Click the OK button to add the document. NOTE.

Deleting documents

To delete a document from your course work list:

a) Select the Manage my Coursework link on your myPDP page.

b) Tick the document's selection box, e.g. Foundation Pharmacy Essay (asthma) [0] view.

c) Click Delete button.

Source: Material provided by Professor K.A. Kane from the School of Pharmacy, University of Strathclyde, Glasgow, Scotland.

Online resources

List of vendors by type: <http://electronicportfolios.com/portfolios/bookmarks.
html#vendors>.

Cotterill, S. J., Horner, P., Hammond, G. R., McDonald, A. M., Drummond, P.,
Teasdale, D., Aiton, J., Orr, G., Bradley, P. M., Jowett, T., Heseltine. L.,
Ingraham, B. and Scougall, K. (2005) 'Implementing ePortfolios: Adapting
technology to suit pedagogy and not vice versa!'. Paper presented at the
ePortfolios 2005 conference, available online at: <www.eportfolios.ac.uk
/FDTL4/docs/fdtl4_docs/Cotterill_et_al_paper_for_eportfolios_2005.doc>.

Jafari, A. (2004) 'The "sticky" eportfolio system: tackling challenges and identifying attributes', EDUCAUSE Review, 39, (4) (July/August 2004): 38–49.
Available online at: <http://www.educause.edu/ir/library /pdf/erm0442.pdf>.

Kraan, W. (2003) 'The Open Source Portfolio initiative', CETIS, available online
at: <http://www.cetis.ac.uk/content/20030820153519>.

Richardson, H. and Ward, R. (2005) 'Developing and implementing a methodol-
ogy for reviewing e-portfolio products', JISC, <www.jisc.ac.uk/uploaded_
documents/epfr.doc>.

Chapter 9

Relating other new technologies to the e-portfolio

Introduction

As we mentioned in Chapter 1, it is hazardous writing about a practice when its development is in such an early stage. There is something of an obsession currently, with the idea that the e-portfolio is a must-have 'tool' within education at all levels. We should stop and question whether or not this 'tool' can live up to everything with which we credit it.

Cohn and Hibbitts (2004) ask, 'where is the body of rigorous, research-based evidence that supports the e-portfolio as a pedagogical and presentational tool? Will the process of developing an e-portfolio stimulate students to engage in reflecting on their learning? How can we measure this? Is it wise to commit the administrative and information communication technology resources to a process that may be operational for only a few years per student? Will it enable the development of a new transformative educational paradigm that more completely integrates education across a lifespan? Will students want to engage with e-portfolios over an extended period, perhaps their entire lives? How will they use them?'

Without doubt the questions posed above will be the subject of research in the future. But how do we proceed in the shorter term? We need to answer some of our questions about e-portfolios by reference to the ways in which related technologies are being used in teaching and learning. What can we discover from these?

We can anticipate that the technologies will move on, and hence the functionality of the e-portfolio will probably be transformed in the future. However, lifelong learning, as a concept, appears to be a given. It is therefore highly likely that we will find ourselves in need of an 'e-portfolio' technological solution to capture learning and learning processes and exchange information about them.

The purpose of this chapter is to highlight other innovative technologies which are currently being used in an educational context. These provide some examples of personal online publishing which directly relate to the potential for e-portfolios. We are starting to see examples of how blogs, wikis and podcasts are being integrated into, or used within higher and further education. Although not as extensive or integrated as e-portfolio systems, they each have some educational attributes in common with them. They can all be used to create artefacts within an e-portfolio. From looking at educational uses and responses to these technologies we can learn something about what to expect from e-portfolios.

Blogs and self-publishing

Blogs can range from very simple personal diaries or journals created by individuals, to complex sites created by institutions and organisations. The term blog is a common abbreviation for the term 'weblog'. The two words are used synonymously. Embrey (2002) suggests that it is 'a cross between a diary, a web site and an online community'. This is an accurate description of many blogs, but the possible definitions are probably as various as the blogs themselves.

The growth in interest in blogs has been astonishing. In 2005, Perseus Development Corp estimated that Google's Blogger had 8 million blogs. Shortly after launching its 'MSN Space' (a form of blog) Microsoft recorded creation of 3 million accounts in 90 days. In 2005 Livejournal claimed to have 6.8 million accounts. There will be some duplication of accounts across these free services, and many accounts will be inactive, but this is still an impressive number of online self-publishers. Blogs may be hard to define but they have become spectacularly popular in the past few years.

Blogs can be broadly categorised as follows:

- Personal blogs, essentially an online journal or diary updated by the author. These may or may not allow comments to be added.
- Personal blogs created as sources of information relating to a particular subject. These are often compiled by an 'expert'. They may be the work of a group operating in a particular field, sharing a particular interest.
- Institutional or organisational blogs that have been created to share information, communicate with customers, assess public opinion, the list goes on ...

What can we hope to learn from blogs? Although generally less formal than e-portfiolios they do possess some of the same features:

- They are organised in a diary form, so could be, and sometimes are, used as a reflective journal.
- They can be made public or private at the discretion of the 'owner'.
- They can include graphics and photographs and can incorporate links to video clips, applications etc.
- They provide a user-friendly interface for publishing content online for users who are largely novices at online publishing.
- They can be used to disseminate information about a person's ideas, beliefs or achievements in the same way as a showcase e-portfolio might.
- The appearance and content can be personalised in the way that we would expect would be possible with certain sorts of e-portfolio.
- The user does not own the system even though they are known as the 'owner' of the blog. They often do not pay directly for the service. Their content is being held by a central organisation from which it is accessed.

Blogs may also incorporate or utilise other technologies, for example: a webcam facility, ability to receive messages from a mobile phone; instant online polls, RSS (Really Simple Syndication) feeds. The use of RSS is particularly important for sites which are extensive and which are intended to be up-to-the-minute. Educational bloggers such as Tony Hirst of the Open University use RSS to provide instant updates automatically 'fed' into his blog rather than manually searching.

As with any other emerging technology, if blogs are to be used as an educational tool to support learning, they will need to demonstrate their use in educational contexts. What their general popularity shows is that they can be used for a wide range of purposes, some serious. They are also popular with a large number of relatively novice users. At least some of those users continue to build on entries into their blogs over an extended period of time, which suggests that users of e-portfolios might be motivated to do the same. A far larger number cease to update their blog. It remains visible but is no longer as informative to readers. We need to understand why this happens – although we should not lose sight of the fact that many blogs were probably never intended to 'last'. The neglected blogs may have been early experiments, which have served their purpose. Their authors could have moved on to other blogs, or simply lost interest.

Blogs are sources of information for students, although those students should be aware of the variable quality, treating them with the same caution as other internet sources. They, or similar equivalents, may also become increasingly important as a communication tool, a part of the user's visible 'identity' online. MySpace (http://www.myspace.com), is currently gaining popularity as an alternative to blogging. It offers free online publishing which is particularly suited to sharing music. A MySpace webpage has been credited with the early success of alternative band The Arctic Monkeys, and through such activity has particular appeal to age groups similar to that of our students. For these young people MySpace provides a useful online venue for sharing their thoughts and achievements with an invisible audience prior to starting an e-portfolio as a student. The question is, can the potential of the blog be harnessed by students? Can learners be empowered through the use of blogs and similar spaces? Do blogs have a place in e-portfolio production and use? What more can they teach us about how e-portfolios might be implemented and used?

Blogs and education

If we focus on the use of blogs in colleges and universities, there are two aspects which educationalists generally consider of importance. Firstly, is the blog necessarily a 'personal webpage'? The second aspect relates to who controls the system. These issues are not usually important to the thousands of bloggers creating new blogs on a daily basis. However, if a blog were to be created for educational purposes within a college or university, it might be desirable for the institution to have ownership rights over the 'blog' and ensure 'posting rights' only to classes of students. The distinction between group and personal blogs also becomes important.

Educational uses of blogs may deviate widely from the norm of 'personal webpage' or journal. A blog could be set up such that a tutor or group of tutors have posting rights – can put materials on the blog for the benefit of the students pursuing a particular course. A variant on this educational group blog would be one where the students do not necessarily have the right to post new materials on to the blog, but are invited to add comments to the postings. Clyde (2002) cites some examples of similar blogs, for example ComLib which was created by students in the Computers and Libraries course at the University of Iceland.

This type of group blog has the advantage of directing the students to a single online space which they hold in common. In contrast, if every student in the class has a separate blog this creates an overhead in commenting by the teacher and peers. We can see that the same would be true of the collective vs individual e-portfolio use. In whole class teaching we might see, use, and develop a group e-portfolio to encourage practice in building and commenting on an e-portfolio. In some contexts tutors might also find operational and teaching advantages in having one collective e-portfolio to which all students refer, or to which all students are expected to contribute. The group project might have a group e-portfolio which details how the project developed over time and collects the experiences and ideas of all participants.

In practice it is relatively unusual for a blog or e-portfolio to be in effect a collectively produced 'publication'. This is more likely to happen with a wiki (see below). If sharing and working collaboratively it is more usual to have a single product (blog or e-portfolio) established by the tutor. This provides a focal point on which students all comment. For assessment purposes it will also clearly be important to know whose work the blog or e-portfolio is, unless it is to be treated as a group or collective assessment.

The concern about who owns the blogging system, raises a number of different issues. Where blogs are used in teaching it is important that they can still be accessed as long as the learning need exists, or at least as long as assessment requires this. The lifespan may be relatively short for class-project blogs or e-portfolios, but it is important that they remain accessible throughout that period. It may also be important to be able to 'lock' the blog at some stage (e.g. assessment cut-off) and prevent further additions and changes. This degree of control and reliability may not be possible if a free external service provider is used. It may also be less possible – certainly less easy – to restrict the audience that can access and/or comment on the blog. For these reasons, largely around robustness and security – the need to guarantee a service and to restrict access to specific groups – blogs used in education are often hosted within the institution using institutional servers. We can expect this to also be the case for most e-portfolio systems, as robustness, persistence and security will also be concerns for these.

One way of looking at a blog used in conjunction with an e-portfolio could be as a means of keeping the portfolio current by archiving material within the e-portfolio. The material remains available for future reference, but only the most recent information is automatically given prominence. Another way to use blogs in conjunction with e-portfolios is to provide wider access, via the blog, to elements within the e-portfolio. The blog could in some cases act as a 'sampler' of the e-portfolios of a class, or as the public window into a student's showcase e-portfolio. It is a way of bringing the world into the student's work and of sharing the work of students more widely. Referring to blogs in the classroom Lohnes (2003) cites Colleen Wheeler, a blogger and member of the Information Technology and Services staff at Wheaton College in Norton Massachusetts:

> weblogs can support many of the critical touch points in the College experience, as a living, reflective journal informing a students' portfolio; a bridge to connect class content and writing assignments; a strategic tool to fuel ongoing research; a collective memory for remote or co-located teams; or a gentle orientation to the new student or employee, providing insight and context into how an unfamiliar community really works.

Sharing beyond the classroom through use of blogs is commented on in the newsletter of the National Institute for Technology and Liberal Education (NITLE) at Ann Arbor. In this Lohnes (2003) writes that weblogs allow users to publicise content to the web from their browser, providing users with an unprecedented ability to participate in the internet community. She believes that the advent of easy-to-use web publishing tools has effectively lowered the technology barrier. Staff and students can take advantage of the promise of the internet as a technology that bridges space and time, cultures and languages and enables communication on a global scale. She talks of bloggers inviting individuals from local, national and international communities to participate in college or university classes via their weblogs.

Blogs and e-portfolios working together can clearly provide a means of opening up the classroom experience for students. It is not difficult to imagine creative and entrepreneurial teachers inviting experts on a subject to make comment on student work through a blog. This could be truly transformative for students. The parallel in offering publication and commenting beyond the classroom is one that we can also see working with some types of e-portfolio.

At its most basic level, a blog, like an e-portfolio, can be used as a simple personal repository. The beauty of the blog is that it can be updated easily and efficiently, both on and off campus, using desktop or mobile computing. While we might hope for the same for e-portfolio interfaces, the blog can be a very attractive intuitive alternative to the e-portfolio where the institutional system is more challenging or technically less accessible. The blog entries could be linked to from within the e-portfolio as some of their many elements. Many blogging systems automatically archive older materials as more content is added, in itself a useful feature. Alternatively, students can sift through their material chronologically and make links connecting postings to the blog which occurred at different times. This use resonates with the trend in convergence of technologies, and affirms the idea of the e-portfolio being a composite of existing facilities and functions.

One of the most relevant aspects of blogging in education – in terms of e-portfolio implementation – is the ability to comment and collaborate as a result of students' showing and sharing ideas and work. Making work-in-progress available to other students and visible to the tutor can have a profound effect. Lohnes (2003) quotes a professor of Political Science using a weblog to promote and facilitate collaborative discussion and dialogue in his class:

> the weblog facilitated much more collaborative learning by students than in previous courses. Students commented on each other's essay drafts and worked in groups on their research projects. The students did a lot of writing without actually realizing how much they had done. For many of them the writing became a 'fun' activity rather than something that was seen as a drudgery or a hurdle to be overcome.

This example could be extended into many subject areas. It is a heartening example of peer interaction and collaborative learning. The sort of learning that is likely to support the development of independent learners (Falchikov, 2005, Stefani, 2005).

The diary/journal format of blogs also mimics some of the function of the reflective e-portfolio. David Carraher from Harvard Law School (undated) describes student weblogs enabling students to keep track of their thinking over time, to pose questions or to receive comments over an extended period. He gives a hypothetical example of a student expressing how he/she initially understood a particular topic or subject, but that a comment by a teacher or another student caused a rethink. By keeping a weblog, the student could link to websites on the topic in question, obtain comments from peers, keep parts of the weblog private, others open for public discussion, or discussion by students only. Although such ideas are remarkably similar to our hopes for e-portfolios, they are not a typical use of blogs. How blogs are used depends on the goals of the course of study. If there is an approach to teaching that encourages learners to generate knowledge and to express their own standpoints openly and continuously then blogs can support this and students are likely to respond well. If the teaching ethos is content-driven and teacher-centred, then blogs (or e-portfolios) will, like any other technologically mediated solution, have their limitations. At worst they could be seen by students as a burden with no real benefit.

The optimistic headline of the National Education Computing Conference (NECC) is that the possibilities for blogs in education are limitless. This conference identified a huge range of uses for the blog in the classroom. (Their website http://web.uoregon.edu/ISTE/NEC C2005 is well worth a visit for anyone thinking of using blogs in teaching and learning).

Again some of the ideas put forward treat the blog as a reflective journal – this time for teachers. NECC suggest that it could help teachers to:

- share ideas for teaching activities to be used in the classroom
- provide tips for beginning teachers
- share classroom technology management technologies.

Using blogs in these ways could be an ideal starting point for colleges and universities that have not yet embarked on a major e-portfolio project. It could help staff and students to recognise how reflective online self-publishing can be helpful to them. The blog could also act as a pilot project to encourage both staff and students to use technology in teaching and learning in a non-threatening, less resource-intensive manner.

What can we expect from blogs?

Creating a blog is very easy to do, as millions of users have now demonstrated. They offer us hope that students could become effective online publishers if given the right e-tools. We can also see that the uses of some blogs is very similar to what we might expect from certain types of e-portfolio. Blogs may offer a route into e-portfolio publishing, or act as a resource within the e-portfolio. While blogs may lack the sophistication of e-portfolios, the advantages are in ease of use and low (or no) cost.

It is likely that your students already have an awareness of blogs and similar spaces. Many will have published or commented on blogs in the past. It should not be too difficult to integrate blogs into teaching and learning, although there will be concerns with doing so. These are issues about control of contributions and control of systems. These same concerns relate to e-portfolio use.

Wikis as works in progress

Wikipedia is probably the best known wiki. This international, web-based, free content encyclopedia describes itself as a 'project', one which has already run for several years and is extremely extensive. Although initially viewed by some with scepticism, Wikipedia is rapidly becoming acknowledged as a useful resource. This is the definition that Wikipedia have offered of a wiki:

> Wiki is a type of website that allows the vistors themselves to easily add, remove, or otherwise edit and change some available content, sometimes without the need for registration. This ease of interaction and operation makes a wiki an effective tool for collaborative authoring.
> Wikipedia, http://www.wikipedia.org (accessed 5 October 2006)

Of course that was the definition of a wiki at the time when we consulted Wikipedia. The content of a wiki is very time-dependant. It is in the nature of wikis that they can change content at short notice. The right to create new entries and edit existing ones is often restricted, but can be open to all and then retrospectively moderated or monitored. Because of this freedom, wiki entries are always to some extent a work-in-progress which can be improved, or at least altered, by any of the permitted editors. According to the What is Wiki? Website (accessed 31 July 2006), 'allowing everyday users to create and edit any page in a web site is exciting in that it encourages democratic use of the web and promotes content composition by non-technical users'.

That level of freedom is not available for all wikis. In *The Wiki Way: Quick Collaboration on the Web*, Leuf and Cunningham (2001) identify six types of wiki based on access:

- The fully accessible and open wiki
- The lockable wiki where all pages are public but not all can be authored
- The gated wiki
- The members only wiki
- The firewalled wiki
- The personal wiki.

The wiki is unusual among group communication mechanisms in that it allows the organisation of contributions to be edited in addition to the content itself. It also allows dispersed communities to work together in an open collaborative online environment. For Wikipedia the community is very large and members of it may have never met, even though they have worked productively together over long periods. For class-based projects, the community may be small and the scope of the wiki restricted.

Wikis, like blogs, have some key characteristics in common with, or of relevance to e-portfolios:

- *Flexibility and simplicity* – content can be created, edited or deleted by users who have little or no technical skill in conventional online publishing. Each page has an edit link and, although conventionally wikis required some knowledge of simple code many now have WYSIWYG (What you see is what you get) editors. This allows input of entries as straight text with formatting selected using icons (as with common word processing packages).
- *Easy linking between pages and to external pages* – each wiki page is a highly connected document. The wiki page is not only easy to change, but also dynamically organised with links to other content.
- *Constant evolution of work* – material is updated regularly, as a work-in-progress. The wiki is generally a work which develops over a period of time. If you visit it in the future there will be differences from how it looks now. The work is becoming more 'finished' and comprehensive all the time.
- *There are many versions* – as part of the evolution there are many versions of the wiki. While only the latest version is displayed as a matter of course, the earlier versions may also have merit. In most wikis the owner or editor can return to and restore earlier versions of the wiki page.
- *Allows for collaborative work* – documents can be collectively authored, regardless of geographical or time boundaries. The commenting of others on the work is a crucial part of the making of the wiki.

Wikis and education

Wikis can be, and have been, used in educational contexts to faciliate asynchronous communication and online group collaboration. Their particular strength is in allowing dispersed groups to work on and develop a single coherent document, or a set of linked documents while giving credit for each person's contribution. The wiki can be used as a composition system, a discussion medium, a repository, a mail system and a tool for collaboration. The use of a wiki in universities and colleges can range from a repository for agreeing meeting notes and setting meeting agendas to experimental instructional approaches. Some institutions are even experimenting with wikis as e-portfolios. When used as a presentation tool, artefacts can be easily shared within a wiki-folio.

A case study from Educause Learning Initiative (ELI, 2006) describes a group of students carrying out a class project. One of the team members suggested using a wiki, having been impressed herself by the ease with which anyone can browse and modify the wiki with nothing more specialised than a web browser. Team members can post rough drafts of work to the wiki and other members can modify it, add to it or change it – either in real time or asynchronously. What was appealing about carrying out this project using the wiki was the fact that work could be carried out any time, any place. A very exciting development for the team was publishing the URL for the team's wiki. The work in progress was in this way put up for public scrutiny by experts in the particular field of work. The feedback was very positive with useful suggestions for new content and potential rewording of some aspects of the project.

Opening up a wiki to public contributions has the potential to gather raw material from diverse sources. At best this can strengthen the wiki by ensuring that the views expressed are not too narrow. It can result in building an authoritative consensus. However it is common within publicly accessible wikis for there to be no quality control or assurance *prior to* publication. As with any data-gathering experience students need to develop good skills in analysing, evaluating, synthesising and selecting appropriate material. If they are managing their own wiki they will probably need additional editorial skills.

As with a blog, the wiki could be used as a learning folio for individuals or groups of students. All the materials and artefacts can be archived and, according to Lamb (2004), wikis work very well as shared online sketchpads or as spaces for brainstorming. They are also well suited to collating and maintaining lists or collections of links to other source materials.

More complex processes can also be supported. For example, at the University of British Columbia (UBC) wikis are being utilised in highly innovative ways throughout the university:

- The Faculty of Applied Science Instructional Support links wikis into its course management system authoring environment so that design teams can quickly and collaboratively build reference lists and course outlines, brainstorm instructional strategies and capture innovative suggestions.

- Staff in The Education Faculty of UBC are using a wiki as a support tool for collaborative experiments in composition and as a prompt for reflection on online reading and writing tasks.
- The Career Services Unit is using a wiki to store and organise content for a major new job posting and career development website.

Other uses of wikis in colleges and universities include:

- The Romantic Audience Project at Bowdon College which is a collaborative study collecting entries focussing on poems, poets and topics related to Romantic literature. The students themselves chose the wiki framework because it was a dynamic and unpredictable means of highlighting particular teams as being representative of communal interest in the study of Romanticism. The wiki allowed collaboration and research highlighting which authors or poems attracted attention and discussion and which did not. This presents a highly creative aspect to teaching and learning.
- At the University of South Florida, a wiki is being used to support writing instruction in the English department. Writing instruction is in fact one of the most common pedagogical applications of wikis. In this context the wiki provides a low cost but effective communication and collaboration tool. The wiki promotes the close reading, revision and tracking of drafts and emphasises writing as an iterative process rather than merely a product-oriented task.

(Lamb, 2004)

Enhancing learning through the use of wikis

If the goal for tertiary education is to enhance student learning and simultaneously embed the use of technology into teaching and learning, the wiki has significant potential as an e-tool. For example, wikis can be used to facilitate computer supported collaborative learning (CSCL). CSCL is defined as the development of collaboration by means of technology to augment education and research. It promotes peer interaction and facilitates the sharing and distribution of knowledge and expertise amongst a group of learners (Lipponen, 2002). Collaborative learning exercises are student centred; they enable students to share authority and they empower learners to build on their foundational knowledge. However, as with any other teaching and learning situation, students need to be made aware of their responsibilities in this type of learning situation.

Wikis used as tools for CSCL can be empowering for students. At their best, wikis are provocative, inspiring, fun and addictive. They can encourage creativity, remove the limits on class time, give teachers a better sense of student understanding and interest and keep students writing, thinking and questioning. Blogs and wikis both have the potential to encourage student participation in more active learning. With the advances in technology users are finding a range of different applications for both of these in education (Kinzie, 2005). In many cases though, teachers are struggling to keep up with the changes being driven by students' innovative uses of the technology. Where this is happening the potential of these e-tools may be limited by resistance to change by university and college staff.

In addition to the change management challenges, there are some difficult issues emerging with regard to libel and intellectual property. Freedom to publish and openness to public contributions, particularly anonymous contributions, are challenging the potential of wikis to become trusted sources. Little research has yet been published on these issues, but with time we can expect to see more focus on the thorny issue of the authentication of materials presented in blogs and wikis.

The pedagogical challenges presented by wikis in the classroom

Wikis can function effectively within a variety of contexts including colleges and universities, but in educational environments they raise some specific issues – notably the issues of security and privacy concerns common within e-learning.

There is currently research being carried out on these issues, though some would argue that addressing these concerns through formal structuring of the wiki and strict 'regulations' will destroy the very essence of the wiki. Other points, which may be more disconcerting for teachers than for students, include the absence of an explicit organising structure in some wikis. If users are more accustomed to hierarchical structure and directed navigation they may initially feel disorientated. Templates or 'scaffolding' may be provided particularly if the wiki is being used in an educational context – but the purists would say that the more design you use in a wiki, the more user functionality you sacrifice (Lamb, 2004).

Tracking work created in wiki spaces can pose some problems. Attribution of individual work can be difficult – and could pose problems for assessment of student work carried out using the wiki. This could impact on how the contribution of individual members of a collaborative group can be defined. Traditional teaching and learning situations often include peer and self-assessment and generate similar problems. Encouraging computer-supported co-operative learning will further emphasise the importance of such assessment strategies. This is a positive move, but staff need to embrace the idea and actively promote it. In very simple terms students can be asked to sign or identify any work they contribute within the wiki. In Kairosnews (a blog), Heather James confesses that using wikis in her teaching was her 'brilliant failure' (Kairosnews, 2004). What she did was to change the tool, rather than change her teaching practice. She failed to recognise the 'great potential of the wiki' to be completely disruptive (in a good way) to the classroom setting. Afterwards she concluded that for the wiki to work at its best, the participants need to be in control of the content. This means that the teacher has to be prepared to give over control to the students.

As Lamb (2004) emphasises, it is a safe bet that wiki-like writing spaces will be featured in future course management systems along with other 'social software' tools and protocols such as blogs – but if teaching practices don't evolve to accommodate such tools, the effects on learning will be superficial at best. Technology is moving at a tremendous pace, yet there is still uncertainty about whether educators, institutions and developers will join in, or simply coexist with what could be revolutionary forces. There is a danger that staff in colleges and universities will try to maintain their familiar and tested approaches in the face of this new technological tide. They could stand their ground, stick with tradition and simply be overrun.

On one level wikis (and blogs) are simply webpages. However wikis and conventional webpages differ in substantial ways. While there are differences between different wikis, they still have many features in common. Table 9.1 summarises the usual differences between webpages and wikis (Arreguin, 2004).

Although there are currently no published examples of wikis as e-portfolios, it is clear from the emerging literature, that the development of the wikifolio is underway. Hence the importance of including reference to wikis in this book. It is also easy to see how wikis, like blogs, can contribute elements within a student e-portfolio. Material from a wiki can be transported into an e-portfolio contributing to the record of student development.

Table 9.1 Key differences between wikis and conventional webpages

Wikis	Conventional webpages
Open editing	Limited editing
Simple text formatting language	Conventional HTML
Earlier versions stored in online database	Earlier versions not automatically stored
Easy to create new pages	Harder to create new pages
Low security	Higher security
Equal user roles	Hierarchical user roles
Multiple anonymous authorship	Limited known authorship
Communal, collaborative	Individual
Pages considered always in process	Pages considered finished

Source: Arreguin, 2004.

Combining technologies – the birth of the podcast

Just as you thought you had kept abreast of some of the key developments in the classroom, another technological solution pops up! This time it is the ability to easily make audio (and sometimes video) recordings available online. The technology we are referring to is known as 'podcasting' because of its early association with online broadcasting and Apple's iPod portable digital MP3 player.

A quick word on a fast-growing technology: podcasting in education

The popularity of MP3 players amongst young people has been tremendous. Ultraportable players are now available which students can feasibly carry with them everywhere. They are wearable computing devices and are emerging as important mobile learning devices (Kukulska-Hulme and Traxler, 2005). Although most students will use MP3 players primarily to listen to and organise their music, more recent and powerful devices now also allow them to view images as stills, slide shows and video. It is also possible to record using MP3 devices and make your own uploadable files, to create your own podcasts. With integration into mobile phones it is possible to take pictures or video and then upload the result to a server while away from the campus computer network. There is enormous educational potential in recording notes and images, and sharing these online, while still 'in the field'. In terms of the e-portfolio it can allow students to 'capture' their reflections as the event happens. It can allow students to accurately record achievements which would otherwise be lost. Because the devices are so small and are relatively affordable they allow every student to make their own personal audio record.

Podcasting is the posting of content, typically in the form of an audio MP3 file, onto the internet. A listener can then download this to their computer or to an MP3 player. The ease with which audio recordings could be made has attracted not only the attention of musicians but also some bloggers. Audio-blogging (providing links to MP3 recordings in blogs) is thought to have originated as early as 2003.

Other features of podcasts include:

- The use of Really Simple Syndication (RSS) technology to subscribe to a 'feed' to automatically receive updates. These could be bulletins or news flashes, or they could be radio programmes or lectures. A service increasingly offered by commercial broadcasters such as the BBC, O'Hear (2005b) in the *Education Guardian* (education.guardian.co.uk) describes podcasting as 'radio' content which a listener subscribes to via the internet. Once subscribed, the listener receives a new podcast as soon as it is available, which can then be played either on a computer or portable MP3 player at a time that suits the listener.

- Accessing (and with some devices creating) files whenever and wherever the user wishes. This is part of the mobile computing aspect of MP3 players. In some further education colleges it has allowed catering students to send to their tutors on-the-job recordings of their culinary achievements via mobile phone (by creating MP3 files of their thoughts and still and video images of the product).

- Reaching international audiences at much faster speeds compared to radio/television which is geographically limited. This is an aspect held in common with many other forms of online publishing. It has been particularly important in allowing wide access to music by unpublished artists.

- Saving and archiving of podcasts by the user. The players usually allow creation of 'playlists' which group related recordings according to the preferences and instructions of the user. Players also allow users to search for recordings by date, title, artist or recent use. The MP3 player becomes in this way an ultra-portable repository of audio recordings. In some institutions these recordings could include lectures.

If there was ever any doubt that students coming in to college or university will arrive with a high degree of technical know-how, this is dispelled by increasingly innovative initiatives in schools. For example, pupils at Musselburgh Grammar School in East Lothian, Scotland produced 'podcast' coverage of a one-day music event held on the school's grounds. Children aged 12–13, with the help of older pupils and teachers, wrote and produced the MGS Podcast as an entertainment and information show for the school and wider community. This podcast project is thought to be the first ever UK school podcast and was short-listed for the New Statesman New Media Award (O'Hear, 2005b).

The *Seattle Times* (October 2005) also reports on teachers using iPods as educational tools, with children in elementary schools making podcasts. More informal uses are in learning languages, for example learning conversational Italian by downloading the tutorials onto an MP3 player. Distance learning has a history of successful use of audio in teaching. Podcasts are in one sense simply the latest manifestation of this. Students can now download recorded sessions onto their players rather than using supplied tapes and CDs.

Campbell (2005) points out that there are a few technicalities in podcasting which need to be addressed. However, these relate to uploading and encoding rather than recording and listening. So for most students the technology is very easy to use. Because of their association with popular music MP3 players are also often already very familiar devices to our students.

What have podcasts got to do with e-portfolios?

It is not difficult to imagine students transferring materials from their MP3 players and mobile phones to their electronic portfolios, or making their own podcasts for inclusion in an e-portfolio. As the recording device is so portable it opens up the potential for students to reflect on learning as this occurs. It is also now easier to capture performances and quickly disseminate this for wider comment.

The newer video-enabled players could provide portable devices for showcasing an e-portfolio to prospective employers. It is not difficult to imagine that some combination of blog and podcast could provide an effective shop window in which a student could display achievements and invite comment. By adding a wiki this could be a group showcase, created and updated collaboratively. All of these technologies are already available to students and we see in MySpace.com examples of their use as informal showcases. Combinations of blogs, wikis and podcasts are already being used by young people to mimic e-portfolios, using open rather than institutional systems and informal rather than formal content. As Campbell points out, many students will have been 'blogging', preparing and editing videos, creating Flash animations, manipulating photographs and recording digital video as part of their leisure activities. The new generation of students has grown up with these technologies at their fingertips. In an educational setting, with the right sort of guidance, with authentic assessment tasks, students can use these technological tools to create powerful, creative work. Imagine engaging students in learning projects which by their very nature encourage teamwork, enterprise skills, technical literacy, writing skills, presentation skills and listening skills?

The learning potential of podcasts

A word of caution is that while many students will arrive at college or university already well versed in how to use new technologies, this may not be the case for all students. In a context of lifelong learning and mass (higher) education, the student population is diverse. One aspect of that diversity may relate to previous access to new technologies. David Baugh talks of the difficulties of teaching students to write for an audience because the audience for students' writing efforts is usually non-existent. An effective podcast which is intended for a public audience doesn't just happen, it usually has to be scripted. To produce material for a podcast, students have to draft and redraft their work and edit the audio. This is just the sort of awareness of audience and refining of content that we would also expect to be necessary across e-portfolios.

Campbell (2005) talks of the power of the human voice and the value of the 'explaining voice'. He believes that the 'explaining voice' conveys microcues of hesitation, pacing and inflection that demonstrates cognition and metacognition. He says 'when we hear someone read with understanding, we participate in that understanding. The explaining voice trains the ear to listen not just for meaning.' He illustrates his point by talking about his own podcasts of John Donne's poems – and how difficult it can be even for a specialist to make sense of some of Donne's poems. Campbell produced a podcast of Donne's poems each day over a period of time, building up a collection of poetry and commentary of five- to eight-minute chunks. This supported his students in preparing for assignments in which they were expected to make comment on, take issue with, and analyse the poems. Campbell explains that doing this was a learning experience for him on his own specialist subject. We can see that if students were required to produce their own podcast readings and comments, this could be even more educationally effective. The best of their work could be included in their e-portfolios.

Podcasts have great potential in educational contexts. However, there is, as with any new technological advance, caution required.

• Podcasting, as one of many user-friendly online publishing technologies, can provide transformative learning experiences in further and higher education, but students may prove to be better at preparing podcasts than their teachers. This provides the opportunity to encourage students to show their creativity, but teachers and tutors need to recognise this shifting dynamic and learn to give their students space to experiment.

• Podcasting as a tool to support learning is dependent on good listening skills. As a learning skill, listening is taken for granted. It will be interesting to capture students' views on podcasts, and how they use them. It will also be worth considering the accessibility issues. Could this be an assistive technology for students who find conventional text-based recording of thoughts problematic? Or will it create problems for hearing impaired students and staff?

• To make or use podcasts access to a computer, an iPod or an MP3 player is essential. While it appears to be the case that everyone owns one or all of these digital devices, it is clearly important to check availability and access arrangements for all of the students in classes where podcasting will be used.

• There is an assessment overhead for teachers. They will now need to listen to content in order to provide feedback and assessment. Skills in skimming text will not translate into reviewing podcasts, and the teaching workload may increase as a result. It could be more difficult to make comparisons and links between elements in a student's audio work. Commenting on audio will, in most disciplines, require new skills for staff. They may choose, in turn, to create audio rather than written feedback on students' work.

The role of new technologies in e-portfolios

Clearly developments in educational technology are ongoing. We are still trying to understand how some of the more recent technologies could be incorporated into teaching and the support of student learning. Keeping up with the pace of technology will stretch most staff and discourage some. However, it has become expected that students graduating from college or university will be competent in the use of new technologies. It is therefore important to experiment with technology in teaching and to understand what it can offer. This is particularly the case when we look at e-portfolios as these will probably collect together many elements generated using new technologies.

The overarching emphasis must be on the pedagogical principles rather than technology for its own sake. We are aware that research remains to be done to ascertain the impact of technology on student learning. Although personal computers have been used in education for over twenty years, and the internet has been part of university and college teaching for a decade, the technology still feels very new and unfamiliar. In part this is because the potential is changing all the time. Both the challenges and the potential of e-learning appear to be limitless. Many now believe, these authors amongst them, that the potential can be harnessed to enhance learning and create new opportunities for learners. E-portfolios may prove to be the focal point for the execution of many new teaching technologies, a melting pot for the blending of e-learning technologies.

Online resources

<http://www.blogger.com>.
<http://wiki.org/wiki.cgi?WhatIsWiki>.
<http://www.wikipedia.org>.
<http://www.bbc.co.uk/radio/downloadtrial/>.

Chapter 10

E-portfolio futures

The aim of this concluding chapter is to consider possible futures for the use of e-portfolios. Where is this practice taking us? What impact might e-portfolios have on our lives – socially, technically and practically? The ultimate purpose of constructing scenarios is that by considering the future, we become more aware of what is going on right now! What choices might we be making now that will shape the use we can make of e-portfolios in the future?

Scenarios are distinctly structured views of the future that are self-consistent and plausible. Scenario planning is a well-honed art, which this chapter does not intend to practise, merely to emulate:

> Scenario planning derives from the observation that, given the impossibility of knowing precisely how the future will play out, a good decision or strategy to adopt is one that plays out well across several possible futures. To find that 'robust' strategy, scenarios are created in plural, such that each scenario diverges markedly from the others. These sets of scenarios are, essentially, specially constructed stories about the future, each one modelling a distinct, plausible world in which we might someday have to live and work.
>
> (Wilkinson, n.d.)

Rather than offering several competing scenarios we have explored here aspects of e-portfolio use to show how they might be perceived in the future by very different users.

Of course, e-portfolio futures are integrally linked to IT practices and developments more generally – security and access issues, applications of collaborative networking, personalisation and customisation, wireless and mobile functioning, and standards and interoperability.

Personal development planning (PDP) is another function which will have an impact on how successful e-portfolios could be in the future. Will employers insist on seeing a PDP or career profile at the hiring stage? And a PDP e-portfolio at annual meetings with each employee? Will universities expect to see a PDP for entry and transfers between institutions?

Finally, ownership is the key to the social acceptance of e-portfolios. Could e-portfolios become ubiquitous and could society ever come to view e-portfolios as just as 'necessary' a technology as mobile phones? Will everyone want to 'own' an e-portfolio?

The scenarios which follow are not idealised, positive stories of a future we know will never come about. Each one contains problems, whether technical, social or practical, yet each takes the application of e-portfolios a step or two beyond current practice and about ten years into the future. The implication in these scenarios is that e-portfolios will be used in social as well as academic and employment areas of our lives.

Scenarios

The following scenarios are intended as illustrative examples of the ways in which e-portfolios might develop in a range of different sectors.

Profile A: The FE Student

- Student in a Further Education College taking a course in design technologies
- Aiming to enter the workplace shortly
- Has an interview with a prospective employer

Story

Toby is preparing a presentation for his job interview by selecting relevant items from his e-portfolio which he has had since he was in primary school. He is aware that the selection of candidates for interview is now largely determined by the e-portfolio that he presents. This is, in effect, his application. He selects a couple of recent assignments along with the grades and teacher's comments. He has some videos of his work while on placement and two video references from staff there. He adds extracts and diagrams (both hand drawn and computer generated) from a project he did last year on designing a robot. In listing his hobbies, he adds photos of the motorbike which he built himself and links to an online forum where he has been active in a community looking at technology in classic science fiction films. He is one of the moderators of the 'Star Trek' forum. He worries that this might appear too 'nerdy' but his college career counsellor advises him to leave it in. Finally he adds the transcript of his secondary school leaving certificate and the list of courses he has taken at college.

It has taken Toby almost a week to select from the many entries within his e-portfolio to create the right look and feel for this employer. He includes links to some of their designs to demonstrate that he has researched the business and tried to link his ideas to theirs. Part of his application will be a diagnostic test, that he will complete if shortlisted for interview. Even if he does not get offered a job he will be given the results of that test. If he scores well he will probably add the test results to his e-portfolio. Toby will also receive feedback from the interview so that he can identify strengths and weaknesses and, if necessary, work these into his reflection and development plan.

The employer is satisfied with Toby's application, and shortlists him for interview. However, after interview they decide not to employ him. As part of their feedback they cite an absence of personal development planning and information on career intentions. This is the weakest area in his e-portfolio. Unfortunately the college he attended did not put much emphasis on PDP until the last year. He now needs to do further work to make a good impression, but it will be very difficult to look back three years and make a case for what he was thinking and planning at that time. As the entries will be time-stamped, any future interview panel will be able to see that this portion of his e-portfolio has been, to a large extent, retro-engineered.

The next employer to which Toby applies has a very different set of requirements. There is a very strict limit to the size of the e-portfolio that can be submitted and a different set of guidelines. He could include the test results from his previous application – these were impressive – but he is obliged to select between different components and already has far too many. He is only allowed one multimedia file and is not sure which to choose.

It seems to him that there is entirely too much flexibility in what an employer expects from the e-portfolio. This is all very hard work. He hopes that he gets a job soon.

Assumptions

The main assumptions are:

1   that students have an extensive store of materials from which to select in preparing presentations;

2   that transcripts and certified grades can be linked from institutions into personal portfolios;
3   that employers expect such presentations when hiring, but each may have different requirements.

Profile B: The University Lecturer

- University lecturer teaching partly face-to-face and partly online
- Aiming for promotion to senior lecturer shortly
- Developing a personal development e-portfolio that provides evidence of research, teaching and contributions to administration

Story

Sarah has maintained her e-portfolio very diligently for some years, entering emails from students and colleagues which praise her work, making links to citation indices of her publications and noting administrative tasks she has completed. She has also kept a reflective journal in which she notes her thoughts on how to improve her teaching, on possible research avenues and personal career aims. Using a new graphics package, she has made a mind map of the elements of her career so far, showing how the teaching and research are mutually supportive.

Last year Sarah decided to include photos of workshops she had led and podcasts of lectures and interviews she had given. Her e-portfolio also contains learning activity and learning design schemas for online learning that she has designed. She was keen to highlight student performance statistics which show the level of interactivity and grades achieved for each section. Although she has included links to all her journal publications (both published and 'in-press') she was particularly keen to show examples of students' work to demonstrate how she has nurtured critical thinking in her classes. Sarah has even negotiated with some current and past students to allow her to link her e-portfolio to theirs. She recognises that her real strength is in teaching, so she has played to that strength. As an e-learning enthusiast she is already very technically competent and was pleased with how she could use multiple media in her e-portfolio to showcase her teaching work, demonstrating what makes it distinctive and effective.

The outcome was not quite as anticipated. The promotion committee were apparently impressed with the range of evidence she provided, but felt that promotion should be based on broad evidence of achievement. They were concerned with the number of research publications, and not very interested in Sarah's reflection, student feedback and personal planning. She definitely 'lost marks' on research.

Their feedback was required to show how Sarah's evidence compares with the 'norm' for promotion to senior lectureship. She quickly realised that the emphasis on her e-portfolio needs to be different. Her next step was to consult an e-portfolio consultant to find out how to make her e-portfolio more convincing. In education this kind of service is still quite new and expensive. This one was recommended by a colleague who decided to get out of teaching and needed a completely new approach in her own e-portfolio. The consultant's advice has helped Sarah to polish and emphasise her previously hidden strengths in research. For example she now shows explicitly the research potential of some of her innovative teaching. She is disappointed that the e-portfolio is so much a strategic game. She realises that she may have been naïve in the emphasis that she placed on teaching and reflection in her previous version.

Assumptions

There are several assumptions in this scenario:

1 that university staff maintain an e-portfolio and have sufficient IT skills to develop multimedia components for them;
2 that academic journals are online and unpublished content can be easily accessed for e-portfolio purposes;
3 that e-portfolios are used for promotion cases;
4 that comparisons can be made between e-portfolios within the same job type and the strength of the candidate's e-portfolio can be ranked or scored;
5 that there may be external consultants who can provide advice – for a fee.

Profile C: The Refugee

- Unemployed refugee
- Trying to find a job within an area where he already has skills
- No existing e-portfolio

Story

Kamal is a refugee in his mid-thirties. He has entered the country legally but with few personal possessions and no employment in place. He is confident that his skills as a hotel manager should make him very employable. He is multilingual and has previously worked overseas in the Middle East and Italy. However his employment over the past five years has been in countries where e-portfolios are not common. He does not have one, and to compound his problems his previous employer is no longer in business. In trying to find a job, he continually runs into the issue of demonstrating his qualifications through an e-portfolio. He thinks it should be sufficient to indicate his skills and tell the employer his background, but so far, he has not been hired.

Kamal has no evidence of his skills, no record of employment and no transcript of his educational achievements. Finally he goes to his local employment centre to get assistance in developing an e-portfolio. They help him to locate information about his past employers and initiate a search for his educational records. They are also able to locate the e-portfolio that he started during his employment in Italy eight years previously. Unfortunately the system he used then is not compatible with the one he is now using so he has to copy rather than directly import the information. He starts his new e-portfolio by listing the jobs he has done in the past and writing a reflective journal describing what he learned from each job. Using a PDP template, he indicates his career aims and how he intends to achieve them. Being able to refer to previous employers and provide links to show what their facilities cover helps build his confidence. Now interviewers will at least be able to see that he has previously worked for substantial enterprises.

At the next employment interview Kamal attends, the employer is so impressed with his thoughtfulness and ability to learn, and his diligence in overcoming his lack of a long term e-portfolio, that he is finally hired. He decides that this time he will retain contact with, and continue to update, his e-portfolio.

Assumptions

The assumptions here are:

1   that lack of an e-portfolio is a serious hindrance to employment;
2   that employers value the ability to learn at least as much as academic qualifications;
3   that e-portfolios can be a vehicle for demonstrating reflection on learning;
4   that e-portfolios will continue to persist for long periods of time and can be accessed in the future by their 'owners'.

Profile D: The University Student

- Student at a university where e-portfolios are integral to the teaching
- Assessment on his programme is by e-portfolio
- He is partially sighted
- He is in the final year of his course

Story

Carl has chosen a programme of study where there are no examinations. All continuous and final testing is by e-portfolio submission. This suits him very well, as he does not work well with a scribe and, even with extra time, he finds the pressure of an examination difficult. He has problems reading even very magnified text unaided. He cannot take exams in the same room as other students as his use of voice recognition and screen readout software would disturb them.

He is very pleased that the e-portfolio format supports all sorts of media. It means that he can dictate his reflections as entries in an audio log. He has also, by working with the departmental technician, managed to use his preferred screen magnification software so that he can read and comment on e-portfolios prepared by other students. On one course he received comments from his teacher at three stages in the development of his final project: the outline of what he wanted to do; the first draft of his work; the final submission. This helped not only in improving his work on that course, but in applying the lessons to the rest of his programme.

On his programme Carl has also been able to work collaboratively on assignments – something his sight often hindered in the past. Using a wiki, he worked in a small group to produce a joint presentation and he has commented on other students' blogs, as was required in another assignment.

Carl is now starting to think about how he will present himself to employers. His tutor has made arrangements for a technician to video him using assistive technologies during a work placement. He hopes that this will help prospective employers see that he can work effectively with only minor adjustments to his workspace.

Assumptions

In this scenario there are several assumptions:

1   that universities would consider abolishing examinations, at least in some subjects;

2   that e-portfolios provide an alternative to continuous and final assessment;
3   that e-portfolios offer preferable alternatives to students with some kinds of disability.

Profile E: The Administrator

*   Administrator in an educational institution
*   Responsible for record keeping and transcripts
*   Facing a security crisis

Story

It has come to the attention of the institution that a past student has used the e-portfolio system to access the examinations and assessment database. He has falsified his grades and used the faked transcript to transfer into Medicine in another university. His actual marks were borderline pass and he would not have gained a place on this new course with his original grades. The validity of other student transcripts is now being questioned and the integrity of the whole institution is at stake, as the media have made a major story out of the incident.

Further investigation has revealed that there is a thriving trade in e-portfolio components. Not just grades are being falsified – some past students have been reinventing their entire e-portfolio by borrowing items from other students. As the e-portfolios in question had already been graded this recycling had not been previously noticed. On courses using e-portfolios several students have expressed concern. Some are suggesting that access to the e-portfolio should be restricted to read-only for past students. Others are boycotting the system entirely and suggesting that with so serious a breach the system should be shut down.

The value of e-portfolios as a vehicle for selecting university entrants or shortlisting students for jobs depends on the reliability of the data they contain. People are starting to talk about going back to 'good old paper,' since online systems are never 100 per cent invulnerable.

Assumptions

The assumptions in this scenario are very simple:

1   that links can be made from personal e-portfolios to the record systems of institutions;

2   that e-portfolio transcripts need to be secure enough to be acceptable evidence for institutions and employers.

Profile F: The Senior Citizen

- Senior citizen
- Preparing a life story to pass on to her grandchildren
- Trying to document events and personal reflections

Story

Just as the elderly are advised to make a will, so they are now encouraged to leave an e-portfolio documenting the major events and thoughts of their lives. These become family heirlooms, used by grandchildren to understand history, make sense of their past and see continuity with the present. Moira did not make much use of ICT in her working life, but a college course has allowed her to brush up on her skills and learn how to use standard e-portfolio software. She knows that her grandchildren save things to their personal e-portfolios all the time, and swap clips and pages from it with strangers. She worries that the information that they have in their e-portfolios is too revealing and, in the wrong hands, could be abused. She much prefers this targeted use of an e-portfolio for a specific purpose and limited audience.

In addition to the clips from the family's digital photo albums, which Moira's family already knows, she goes online to the local library to find photos and reports of significant events. She enjoys preparing her own video and audio commentaries, and writes an online journal of her memories and reflections. Picking up one idea from her friends she is now constructing a family tree listing dates of birth, marriages and deaths of her extended family. Photos are added as well as links to various archives and websites documenting how the family left Europe in the nineteenth century and went to Australia. On her holiday next year Moira is hoping to be able to visit the village where her own grandmother grew up. If possible she would like to include video of the house where her father was born and some 'interviews' with anyone who may have known him.

It is very disappointing that Moira cannot use material deposited in her elder sister's e-portfolio only eight years ago. She has been unable to access or link to that record because that style of e-portfolio is no longer used. There was a general problem of incompatibility and competing systems in the early years, but the newer systems are interoperable. The college is trying to find a solution to her problem. Moira is not the only course participant who is affected.

Assumptions

There are several assumptions contained within this scenario:

1   that e-portfolios become ubiquitous as lifelong records, much as photos and diaries are now;
2   that e-portfolio systems are available for everyone in the community;
3   that all ages make use of e-portfolios for sharing personal information;
4   that interfacing with legacy materials continues to be a problem.

Conclusion

These scenarios have drawn attention to a number of technical, social and practical issues which may promote or hinder e-portfolio developments in the future. In fact, elements from all of these scenarios could be enacted today – they are not so futuristic as to be unrealistic.

They reflect themes developed throughout the book:

•   The development and application of e-portfolios is at an early stage and could become rather different in the future. If the original development of the telephone was initially thought to be useful for transmitting opera, what might e-portfolios be used for in the future?
•   Interoperability is key to the long-term functioning of e-portfolios. If educational institutions have proprietary systems which are only useful while students are registered, there will not be widespread diffusion of e-portfolios.
•   Career planning and personal development are lifelong pursuits that e-portfolios help to formalise and encourage.

However, there are several questions which emerge from these scenarios, and they conclude the book on a reflective note appropriate to the whole purpose of e-portfolios:

•   Are lifelong e-portfolios really feasible technically, considering issues of security and future-proofing?
•   Will individuals take responsibility for maintaining an e-portfolio in order to realise the benefits over a lifetime?

- Do we want e-portfolios to become a kind of ID card whereby education, employment and indeed one's personal history is dependent on it and defined by it?

We conclude with a question from Howard Rheingold, a well known techno-futurist:

> If the citizens of the early twentieth century had paid more attention to the ways horseless carriages were changing their lives, could they have found ways to embrace the freedom, power, and convenience of automobiles without reordering their grandchildren's habitat in ugly ways? Before we start wearing our computers and digitizing our cities, can the generations of the early twenty-first century imagine what questions our grandchildren will wish we had asked today? Technology practices that might change the way we think are particularly worthy of critical scrutiny: High-resolution screens and broadband communication channels aren't widget-making machinery but sense-capturing, imagination-stimulating, opinion-shaping machinery.
>
> (Rheingold, 2002, pp.103–104)

Online resources

Aalderink, W. and Veugelers, M. (2005) E-portfolios in the Netherlands: Stimulus for educational change and lifelong learning. Available online at: <www.icto.ic.uva.nl/surf/nl_portfolio/Publicaties/Downloads/aalderink_veu gelers_2005.pdf>.

Gibson, D. and Barrett, H. (2003) 'Directions in electronic portfolio development', Contemporary Issues in Technology and Teacher Education, (Online serial), 2(4). Available: <http://www.citejournal.org/vol2/iss4/general/article3 .cfm>.

Insight: School Innovation: E-portfolio Scenarios. Available online at: <http://insight.eun.org/ww/en/pub/insight/school_innovation/eportfolio_scenarios.htm>.

University of Oxford: Work Task Scenarios. Available online at: <http://www.ict.ox.ac.uk/strategy/worktasks/k/SG-WT-K-05_scenarios_2.xml.

Glossary

Accessibility A characteristic of a tool or system that enables people with disabilities to use it. An accessible website could be navigated by users with visual, hearing, motor, or cognitive impairments. Accessible design can also benefit people with older or slower software and hardware.

Affordance Property of an object, environment, or tool that indicates how to interface with it. (An empty space within an open doorway affords movement across that space.)

Assistive technologies Technology used by individuals with disabilities in order to perform functions that might otherwise be difficult or impossible.

Asynchronous communication Communication which occurs intermittently rather than in 'real time'. An example used in this series is online forums where students can read and respond to messages some time after the message was posted. Another very familiar example is email.

Audioconferencing Communication between two or more sites using standard telephone lines to allow participants to hear and speak to each other.

Blended learning Learning which combines different technologies, in particular a combination of traditional (e.g. face-to-face instruction) and online teaching approaches and media.

Blog (Weblog) An easy-to-publish website consisting of entries posted in date order. Blogs can contain links, images, sound and video (sometimes called *vlogs*). Blogs are usually personal but may invite comments from a wide audience.

Bookmark A way of noting a link using browser software. Bookmarking allows users to return to webpages quickly without remembering or searching for the *URLs,* for quick and easy retrieval. See also *Social Bookmarking.*

Broadband   A means of allowing high speed transmission of data and therefore a quicker connection to the internet than dial-up modems would allow. This permits learning and teaching at a distance using audio and video without lengthy waits for files to download.

Browser   An application such as Firefox or Internet Explorer that displays webpages in a user-friendly graphical format. Browser software may also be used to navigate and display the contents of a personal computer.

Chat   Real-time text-based communication, usually on a one-to-one or small group basis. Chat can be used in e-learning for students to ask questions of peers or the instructor as they work through problems. It is often used to describe *instant messaging (IM).*

Chat room   A virtual meeting space used for real-time text (*chat*) discussions amongst several users.

Collaborative knowledge construction   Collaborative development of an awareness and understanding of facts, truths or information gained in the form of experience or learning (see *Knowledge construction*).

Computer conferencing   Forums on the internet or an intranet where users can post messages for others to read (other terms include discussion boards or bulletin boards).

Constructivism   A philosophy of learning founded on the premise that, by reflecting on our experiences, we construct our own understanding of the world.

Continuing education   Courses designed for part-time adult learners.

Continuing professional development (CPD)   Work-related training or updating which is required to maintain professional standing. This may take the form of formal courses provided, or accredited, by colleges and universities.

Convergence   A way of describing the combination of separate digital information formats, such as text, audio, and video, into new integrated forms. *Podcasting* is an example of convergence between audio broadcasting and personal *MP3* players.

Courseware   Instruction or education delivered as courses using a software program. Can be delivered online or using disks, CD-ROMs and DVDs.

Data mining   Analysing data relating to online activity to identify patterns and establish relationships.

Delivery   Any method of transferring content to learners. This can be face-to-face (traditional) delivery or at a distance. In either case it may include use of the internet, DVDs, CD-ROM, books, and other media.

Dial-up   A way of accessing the internet using a device called a modem. This allows a computer to connect using a phone line. The connection speed is much slower than for *Broadband.*

Digital divide   A term used to describe the gap that exists between those who can afford technology (or can afford the best/fastest technology) and those who cannot.

Distance education or **Distance learning**   Teaching where the student is separated by time or location from the teacher and, usually, other students. Courses are delivered using a variety of synchronous or asynchronous technologies. The Open University is an example of a distance teaching university, but many traditional colleges and universities offer some of their courses 'at a distance'.

Download   Transfer of a file to a user's computer from another connected computer or service, usually using the internet. Download time refers to the amount of time taken to complete a file download. For large (e.g. media) files this could be significant, hence the use of *streaming media.*

e-Administration   Electronic administration. This term covers a wide set of course management applications which take place online, e.g. registration of students, reservation of library books.

e-Content   Refers to the electronic content of a course. Covers a wide range of resources for learning, from specifically created *learning objects* to the content of a third party.

e-Learning   Broad term used to describe electronic teaching and learning using computers, usually through access to online materials or the internet.

Electronic learning environment – An integrated set of electronic teaching and learning tools which combine to form a learning environment (similar to a content management system (CMS), virtual learning environment (VLE), managed learning environment (MLE) and learning management system (LMS)).

e-Portfolio   A collection of electronic files used to support development, dissemination, reflection and/or assessment. Often uses a specialised system for managing and displaying the files and can be accessed once the course is over, or away from campus.

E-tool   Term used to describe electronic software or hardware tools. Examples of software e-tools range from Microsoft *Word* or *Skype* to *Google.* Hardware e-tools include phones, DVD players, iPods etc.

Experiential learning Learning through experience, either in a real situation, such as a workplace, or in a simulation or role play.

f2f (face-to-face) Used to describe synchronous interaction between students or students and teachers within the same space. An example is the traditional classroom setting.

FAQs Abbreviation of 'frequently asked questions' – a format for presenting information as a list of questions with answers. FAQs often appear on websites and may be used as a way of answering anticipated student queries such as 'How do I get a password for the network?'

Formative assessment Assessment intended to give students feedback on their learning progress and to give the teacher an indication of students' areas of difficulty. *MCQs* are a popular way of providing formative assessment within e-learning.

Further education (FE) Post-compulsory education offered by colleges. The 'FE sector' includes tertiary colleges, agricultural colleges, and sixth form colleges.

GB (gigabyte) Just over one billion bytes. 1,000 megabytes.

Google – A very well known example of a **search engine**. The term 'googling' refers to searching the web using any search engine.

Granularity – The size of a learning resource. The smaller the resource, the higher the level of granularity.

Higher Education (HE) University level education, usually leading to the award of a degree.

Higher Education Academy (HEA) The professional organisation of higher education teachers in the UK. HEA aims to help institutions, discipline groups and all staff provide the best possible learning experience for their students.

HTML (Hypertext Markup Language) The programming language used to create documents for display on the World Wide Web.

ICT (Information and Communication Technology) A catch-all phrase used to describe a range of technologies for gathering, storing, retrieving, processing, analysing and transmitting information. The emphasis is on communication, differentiating it from *IT (Information Technology).*

Informal learning Informal learning activities that take place without a teacher and may also take place outside the classroom.

Instant messaging (IM) An application which can be installed to let users '*chat*' to others, sending short text messages to selected 'buddies' (e.g. friends, colleagues or fellow students) who are online. MSN (Microsoft Network) is a popular instant messaging system.

iPod   The brand name of Apple's MP3 player. Often used as a generic term to describe all MP3 players. Gave rise to the term *podcasting.*

Interoperability   When hardware or software is 'interoperable' it has been designed to work with other systems effectively. Interoperability improves the opportunities for reuse and also underpins *mobile learning.*

IT (Information Technology)   In education this term is usually used to describe the use of computers and often refers to the technical skills (IT skills) to use them.

JISC (Joint Information Systems Committee)   A strategic advisory committee working on behalf of UK higher and further education that aims to promote innovative applications of information technologies and systems.

Just-in-time   Characteristic of e-learning which means that learners are able to access the information they need exactly when they need it. This approach is particularly popular in *work-based learning* and training.

Knowledge construction   Building an awareness and understanding of facts, truths or information gained in the form of experience or learning (see *Collaborative knowledge construction*).

Learning environment   The physical or virtual setting in which learning takes place.

Learning object (LO)   Sometimes referred to as a reusable learning object (RLO). A learning object is a digital piece of learning material that addresses a clearly identifiable topic or learning outcome and has the potential to be reused in different contexts.

Learning object economy   Activities related to the production, sharing, distribution and/or reuse of learning resources.

Learning objective   A statement which sets out a measurable outcome of the learning. May be used within a course description. See also *Learning outcome.*

Learning outcome   Statement of what a learner is expected to know, understand or be able to do at the end of a period of learning.

Link   An icon, text or image within a webpage which if clicked will display another webpage, or resource. Used in the design of hypertext. A set of linked webpages is a website.

M-learning or **mobile learning**   Teaching and learning using technologies such as mobile phones, PDAs, wireless notebook computers or MP3 players.

Multiple choice questions (MCQs)   Questions where the learner selects from a number of choices as answers. Some MCQ software will allow construction of mazes or crosswords.

Metadata   Information (data) about a resource which is used to classify and describe it (e.g. name of author, when created). Standards exist for writing metadata which aim to make its use consistent and helpful for retrieval and reuse. A *Repository* will include resources with metadata attached. The metadata will help to locate usable and relevant resources.

MP3   A format for audio file compression that allows users to download or upload recordings over the internet. These files can be organised, stored and played back (or recorded) using an MP3 player or conventional laptop or desktop computers.

Multimedia   An approach to creating material which combines more than one medium (e.g. text and pictures). Can range from a simple slideshow to a complex computer game.

Navigation   This describes the process of moving through a series of pages, either those that are connected to the same site, or pages from separate sites which are linked together.

Netiquette   Etiquette for 'net' users. Suggested or required rules of conduct for online or internet users.

Online   When a computer is connected to another computer via a network. Also used in e-learning to describe being connected to the internet as in 'Now go online and ...'.

Online learning   Refers to learning delivered using internet-based technologies. Also sometimes described as web-based or internet-based.

Open courseware   Courseware or learning resources which are made available free-of-charge, often with some educational licensing restrictions.

Open source software   Software for which the original code is made available free-of-charge so that users can access, modify, and republish it. The Linux operating system is an example of open source software.

PDA (personal digital assistant)   An ultra-portable handheld computer commonly used to organise personal information such as contacts, schedules, etc. Can also be used to display electronic texts, to browse the internet, complete tests and to take notes.

PDF or .pdf (portable document format)   Adobe document file format which allows documents to be displayed with fonts, images, links, and layouts as they were originally designed.

Personalisation or **Personalised learning**   Tailoring content within a course, and/or student support, so that it reflects the requirements or preferences of the individual user. Can be informed by *Student tracking*.

Podcasting   A method of uploading and publishing audio files to the internet. Many podcast services allow users to subscribe to a feed and receive new files automatically by subscription. Outside of education this may be a free service provided by broadcasters, e.g. the BBC.

Real-time communication   Communication in which there is no obvious delay between the time when information is sent and when it is received. Characteristic of synchronous learning, this describes communication which can be close to conventional face-to-face conversation.

Repository   An electronic database of materials together with detailed information (metadata) about them which helps users classify and identify the contents. Contents can be learning resources deposited for reuse, or research, or other documents deposited for dissemination.

Repurpose   To change content by revising or restructuring it so that it can be used for a different purpose or in a different way. Updating is a very light level of repurposing.

Reusable   E-learning content that has been developed to be usable in more than one context or for more than one cohort. This may include a special format (see *Learning object*) which allows import into different systems or delivery mechanisms, usually without the need to make changes to the resource.

RSS feeds   A form of 'news feed' used for supplying (serving) users frequently updated content and increasingly used as a means of automatically updating blogs and other frequently revised sites.

Scalability   The degree to which something (cohort size, computer application, etc.) can be expanded in volume and continue to work effectively.

Screen reader   Computer software that can be used to read aloud content displayed as text on the screen. This may be used as *assistive technology* by some disabled students.

Scroll   To navigate around the screen by moving through text and images on a computer screen in a constant direction, e.g. down, up, right, or left.

Search engine   Software that helps users to locate webpages based on a search of keywords. The search engines maintain databases of websites and use programs (often referred to as 'spiders' or 'robots') to collect information, which is then indexed by the search engine. The most commonly used search engine is Google (www.google.com).

Skype A form of VoIP (voice over Internet Protocol) where voice is transmitted digitally. Can be used to avoid fees charged by telephone companies.

Social bookmarking A form of *social software* which allows users to build sets of annotated bookmarks and share information about these with others. Systems such as del.icio.us (http://www.del.icio.us) can identify common 'tags' (descriptions) used to describe bookmarks and can flag up popular or linked themes.

Social software Software that allows users to connect or collaborate by use of a computer network and encourages sharing and commenting on content. Commonly used examples are MySpace (www.myspace.com) and youtube (www.youtube.com).

Spam Unsolicited junk email, usually offering products or services.

Standard A specification established as a model for some element of e-learning by an authority (e.g. the International Standards Organization (ISO)). E-learning standards are usually aimed at ensuring quality, consistency, and interoperability.

Student tracking The use of software to monitor the progress of a learner through courseware. This data can be used to analyse the effectiveness of a course or environment.

Summative assessment The process of evaluating (and grading) the learning of students at a point in time.

Synchronous learning A real-time learning event. If online rather than *face-to-face* it requires all participants to be logged on at the same time so that they can communicate with each other. Interaction may occur via text, audio or videoconferencing, internet telephony, or two-way live broadcasts.

Thread A related set of messages on a particular topic posted within a computer conference or forum.

Upload To send a file from your computer to another (e.g. as an email attachment), or to publish a file on a webpage.

URL (uniform resource locator) The unique address of an individual webpage or the address of a website, for example http://www.open.ac.uk (The Open University).

Usability The measure of how effectively, efficiently, and easily a person can navigate an interface, find information on it, and achieve his or her goals.

Videoconferencing Using video and audio to allow synchronous communication between participants at different locations. This can be based on a personal computer (desktop videoconferencing), for use as needed, or it can be located at a particular site as a fixture.

Virtual   Not physical. Usually used to refer to something which is happening online – for example a virtual lecture.

Webcast   A way of transmitting video via the web that allows the content to be viewed as it 'streams' so that users do not need to download large files. To receive lengthy streamed webcast it is usually necessary to have a fast computer connection (see *broadband*).

Web conference   A virtual meeting of participants from different locations. Communication can occur using text, audio, video, or a combination of these. Used in contrast to *computer conferencing* (which refers to text-based online forums).

Wireless or Wi-fi (wireless fidelity)   A means of connecting to the internet which relies upon radio-based systems. A 'wired' classroom or building will allow students and teachers within that space to connect to the internet using wi-fi devices without the need to make a physical (cable) connection.

Wiki   A website or similar online resource which allows users to add and edit content collectively. A well known example is Wikipedia (http://wikipedia.org).

Work-based learning (WBL)   Courses which may or may not include classroom components but will integrate a range of learning activities that focus on work-based problems, learning resources sourced from the workplace, times and places for learning (with an emphasis on activities being carried out in the workplace), and different ways that learners work and network together.

WYSIWYG (what you see is what you get)   Pronounced 'wizzy wig', a WYSIWYG program allows users to see text and graphics on screen exactly as they will appear when printed out or published online. It allows users to format text without using programming code.

References

Acker, S. (2005) 'Overcoming obstacles to e-portfolio assessment', *Campus Technology* newsletter: Technology-Enabled Teaching/e-Learning Dialogue. Available at: <http://www.campustechnology.com/article.asp?id=107888 typeid=155>.

Ali, L. (2001) 'Personal development planning in the Faculty of Arts', in C. Juwah, L.A.J. Stefani, J. Westwood, C. Gray and J. Drysdale (eds) *Personal Development Planning in Practice: A Series of Case Studies*. Aberdeen: CLASS, 42–45.

Alverno College: online at: <http://www.alverno.edu/academic/dpp.html>.

Arreguin, C. (2004) 'Wikis', in B. Hoffman (ed.) *Encyclopaedia of Educational Technology*. Available online at: <http://coe.sdsu.edu/eet/Articles/wikis/start.htm> (accessed 26 May 2006).

Attwell, G. (2005) *Recognising Learning: Educational and Pedagogic Issues in ePortfolios*. Available online at: <http://elgg.net/gattwell/files/486/1465/epo rtfoliopaper.doc> (accessed 01 December 2005).

Bangert, A. (2004) 'The seven principles of good practice: a framework for evaluating on-line teaching'. *The Internet and Higher Education,* 7(3), 217–232.

Banks, B. (2004) E-portfolios: Their uses and benefits, 3–12. Available online at: <http://ferl.becta.org.uk/display.cfm?resID=8089> (accessed 4 Jan 2007).

Barnett, R. (1994) *The Idea of Higher Education*. Buckingham: SRHE / Open University Press.

Barrett, H. and Carney, J. (2005) 'Conflicting paradigms and competing purposes in electronic portfolio development' (submitted to *Educational Assessment Journal* 2005). Available online at: <http://electronicportfolios.com/portfo lios/LEAJournal-Barrett-Carney.pdf> (accessed 4 January 2007) .

Batson, T. (2005) 'The electronic portfolio boom: what's it all about?' *Campus Technology*. Available online at: <http://www.campustechnology.com/article.asp?id=6984> (accessed 25 October 2005).

Baugh, D. quoted in O'Hear, S. (2005b) 'Podcasts offer the audience pupils crave', *Education Guardian*. Available online at: <http://education.guardian.co.uk/elearning/story/0,1583830,00.html> (accessed 14 August 2006).

Baume, D. and Yorke, M. (2002) 'The reliability of assessment by portfolio on a course to develop and accredit teaching in Higher Education'. *Studies in Higher Education* 27(1): 7–25.

Bennett, Y. (1993) 'The validity and reliability of assessments and self assessments of work-based learning', *Assessment and Evaluation in Higher Education* 18(2): 83–94.

Biggs, J. (1999) *Teaching for Quality Learning at University*. Buckingham: SRHE/Open University Press.

Bohman, P. (2003) 'Introduction to web accessibility', *WebAIM: 'Web accessibility in mind*, 1–6. Available online at: <http://www.webaim.org/intro>.

Boud, D. (1995) *Enhancing Learning Through Self-Assessment*. London: Kogan Page.

Breivik, P.S. (1998) *Student Learning in the Information Age*. American Council on Education: Oryx Press.

Britain, S. and Liber, O. (1999) *A Framework for Pedagogical Evaluation of Virtual Learning Environments*. JTAP, JISC Technology Applications. Available online at: <http://www.jtap.ac.uk/> (accessed 10 February 2006).

Brown, S. and Glasser, A. (eds) (1999) *Assessment Matters in Higher Education: Choosing and Using Diverse Approaches*. Buckingham: SRHE/OU Press.

Burgess, R. (2005) *The UK Honours Degree: Provision of Information,* the Measuring and Recording Student Achievement Steering Group Consultation Paper, issued by Universities UK and the Standing Conference of Principals. Available online at: <http://www.scop.ac.uk/UploadFolder/open/news/classification.pdf> (accessed 14 August 2006).

Cambridge, B. (ed.) (2001) *Electronic Portfolios: Emerging Practices in Student, Faculty and Institutional Learning*. Washington, DC: Stylus Publishing.

Campbell, G. (2005) 'There's something in the air: podcasting in education', *EDUCAUSE Review* 40(6): 32–47.

Carraher, D. *Weblogs In Education*. Available online at: <http://blogs.law.harvard.edu/carraher/stories/storyReader$6> (accessed 07 August 2006).

Centre for Recording Achievement: e-Portfolios, Personal Development Planning and Recording Achievement. Available online at: <http://www.recordingachievement.org> (accessed 22 May 2006).

Challis, M. (1999) 'AMEE Medical Education Guide no 11 (revised): portfolio based learning and assessment in medical education'. *Medical Teacher* 21(4): 370–386.

Chen, G.D., Liu, C.C., Ou, K.L. and Lin, M.S. (2002). 'Web Learning Portfolio: A Tool for Supporting Performance Awareness', *Innovation in Education and Teaching International,* 38(1): 19–30.

Clyde, A. (2002) 'Shall we blog?' *Teacher Librarian* 30(1): 44–46.

Cohn, E.R. and Hibbitts, B.J. (2004) *Beyond the Electronic Portfolio: A Lifetime Personal Web Space*. Available online at: <http://www.educause.edu/apps/eg/egm04/egm0441.asp> (accessed 28 April 2006).

Collis, B (2005) 'The contributing student: A blend of pedagogy and technology', in J. Copsey (ed.) *The Next Wave of Collaboration*. Auckland, New Zealand: Educause and The University of Auckland Library, 7–12.

Cotterill, S.J., MacDonald, A.M., Drummond, P. and Hammond, G.R. (2004) 'Design, implementation and evaluation of a "generic" e-portfolio: The Newcastle Experience', Proceedings e-Portfolios 2004 ISBN 2–9524576–0-3. Available online at: <http://www.eportfolios.ac.uk/FDTL4/docs> (accessed 10 September 2005).

Dalhousie University (n.d.) *My.ePortfolio*. Availble online at: <http://channel-content.dal.ca/portfolio/sm_writegoals.html> (accessed 22 December 2005).

Developing a Teaching Portfolio, Faculty and Teaching Associate Development (FTAD), Ohio State University. Available online at: <http://ftad.osu.edu/portfolio>.

DfES (2005) E-Strategy, Harnessing Technology: Transforming learning and children's services. DfES: London.

Di Biase, D. with contributions by Zembal-Saul, C., Sabre, J., Howard, D., Rademacher, H., Burlingame, P, Melander, G., Schall, J., Spielvogel, E., Mathews, J. and Orndorff, R. (2002) *Using e-Portfolios at Penn State to Enhance Student Learning: Status, Prospects and Strategies*. E-education Institute, The Pennsylvania State University. Available online at: <https://www.e-education.psu.edu/portfolios/e-port_report.sthml> (accessed 5 January 2007).

Downes, S. (2006) The Students' Own Education. Webcast seminar at Knowledge Media Institute, The Open University, Milton Keynes (5 June).

EDNER (2002) *Formative Evaluation of the Distributed National Electronic Resource Project 2002*. 'Web accessibility issues for higher and further education'. Issue Paper 6. Available online at: <http:/www.cerlim.ac.uk/edner/ip/ip 06. rtf>.

Educause Learning Initiative: Advancing Learning through IT Innovation. Available online at: <http://www.educause.edu/eli>.

Ehrmann, S. (2004) *A Guide to Electronic Portfolio Initiatives – Planning and Formative Evaluation*. Available online at: <http://www.tltgroup.org/programs /Flashlight/FL_Handbook/ePort_Strat.htm (accessed 21 December 2005).

Eklund, J., Kay, M. and Lynch, H. (2003) 'E-learning: emerging issues and key trends'. Australian Flexible Learning Framework discussion paper. Available online at: <http://www.flexiblelearning.net.au>.

e-Learning Centre. Available online at: <http://www.e-learningcentre.co.uk/ eclipse/Resources/accessible.htm> (accessed 01 February 2006).

Elton, L. (2003) *Seven Pillars of Assessment Wisdom*. LTSN Generic Centre.

Elton, L. and Johnston, G.S. (2002) *Assessment in Universities: A Critical Review of Research*. Higher Education Academy, LTSN Generic Centre. Available online at: <http://www.materials.ac.uk/guides/assessing.asp>.

Embrey, T. (2002) 'You blog, we blog: a guide to how teacher librarians can use weblogs to build communication and research skills', *Teacher Librarian* December, 30(2): 7–9.

EPICC (European Portfolio Initiatives Co-ordination Committee) (2006) Available online at: <http://www.eife-l.org/activities/projects/epicc/> (accessed 28 May 2006).

Eportaro. Available online at:<http://www.eportaro.com/index.html>.

Essop, S. (2004) Northern College, *Good Practice in Teaching and Learning.* Available online at: <http://www.northern.ac.uk/papers/guidetogoodpractice/key_skills.html> (accessed 29 May 2006).

Falchikov, N. (2005) *Improving Assessment through Student Involvement.* London: Routledge Falmer.

Garrison, D.R. and Anderson, T. (2003) *E-learning in the 21st Century: A Framework for Research and Practice.* London: Routledge Falmer.

Gathercoal, P., Love, D., Bryde, B. and McKean, G. (2002) 'On implementing web-based electronic portfolios', *Educause Quarterly,* 25(2): 29–37. Available online at: <http://www.educause.edu/ir/library/pdf/Eqm0224.pdf> (accessed 10 November 2005).

Graham, A. (2005) 'Recognising learning: Educational and pedagogic issues in e-porfolios'. Paper presented at *ePortfolio 2005,* Cambridge, October 26–8, 119–127.

Gunn, C. and Harper, A. (2006) 'Using e-learning to transform large class teaching', in M. Bullen and D. James (eds) *Making the Transition to e-Learning: Strategies and Issues.* Pennsylvania: Idea Group Publishing.

Hammond, J. and Stefani, L.A.J. (2001) 'Moving towards an inclusive curriculum at the Glasgow School of Art', *The Skill Journal* 71, 3–9.

Hatton, N. and Smith, D. (1995) 'Facilitating reflection: issues and research'. *Forum of Education* 50(1): 49–65.

Herman, J., Aschbacher, P. and Winters, L. (1992) *A Practical Guide to Alternative Assessment,* Alexandria, VA: Association for Supervision and Curriculum Development.

Herrington, J. and Oliver, R. (2002) 'Designing for reflection in online courses'. HERDSA 2002, 313–319. Available online at: <http://elrond.scam.ecu.edu.au/oliver/2002/HerringtonJ.pdf> (accessed 22 December 2005).

Hopkins, L. (ed.) (2000) *Library Services for Visually Impaired People: A Manual of Best Practice.* Resource: the Council for Museums, Archives and Libraries, 2000. Library and Information Commission Research Report 7b. STV/LIC Programme Report 10.

IMS Global Learning Consortium, Inc. Available online at: <http://www.ims-global.org>.

Ingraham, B. and Bradburn, E. (2003) *Sit Back and Relax: A Guide to Producing Readable, Accessible Onscreen Text.* Available online at: <http://readability.tees.ac.uk> (accessed 10 February 2006).

Jackson, N.J. (2003) 'Nurturing creativity through an imaginative curriculum'. *Educational Developments* 4(2): 8–12. Online updated version, *Creativity in Higher Education.* Available online at: <http://www.heacademy.ac.uk/creativity.htm> (accessed 01 May 2006).

Jafari, A. and Kaufman, C. (2006) *Handbook of Research on ePortfolios.* London: Idea Group Reference.

James, R., McInnis, C. and Devlin, M. (2002) *Assessing Learning in Australian Universities.* Victoria Centre for the Study of Higher Education, University of Melbourne.

Jenkins, M. (2004) 'Unfulfilled promise: formative assessment using computer-aided assessment', *Learning and Teaching in Higher Education* Issue 1: 67–80.

Johnston, B.S. (2004) 'Summative assessment of portfolios: an examination of different approaches to agreement over outcomes', *Studies in Higher Education* 29(3): 395–412.

Jorum Online Repository Service for Teaching and Support Staff in UK Further and Higher Education. Available online at: <http://www.jorum.ac.uk>.

Juwah, C., Stefani, L.A.J., Westwood, J., Gray, C. and Drysdale, J. (eds) (2001) *Personal Development Planning in Practice: A Series of Case Studies,* Aberdeen: CLASS.

Kairosnews (2004) 'A weblog for discussing rhetoric, technology and pedagogy: e-portfolios: does the e mean "exploitation?"', Barton, M. Available online at: <http://kairosnews.org/node/3833> (accessed 20 October 2005).

Kane, K. (2005) Personal communication on pharmacy portfolios.

Kinzie, S. (2005) 'Blogging clicks with colleges', *Washington Post* 11 March 2005, p.B01. Available online at: <http://WashingtonPost.com/wp-dyn/articles/A25305–2005Mar10.html>.

Knight, P.T. (2002) *Being a Teacher in Higher Education.* Buckingham: SRHE / Open University Press.

Kukulska-Hulme, A. and Traxler, J. (2005) *Mobile Learning: A Handbook for Educators and Trainers.* London: Routledge.

Lamb, B. (2004) 'Insurgence emergence convergence', *Educause Review* 39(5). Available online at: <http://www.educause.edu/pub/er/erm04/erm0453.asp>.

Law, D. (2000) 'Information policy for a new millennium', *Library Review* 49(7): 322–330.

Leuf, B. and Cunningham, W. (2001) *The Wiki Way: Quick Collaboration on the Web.* Upper Saddle River, NJ: Addison Wesley.

Lipponen, L. (2002) *Exploring Foundations for Computer-Supported Collaborative Learning.* CSCL 2002, Boulder, CO: Laurence Erbaum Associates Inc.

Little, J.W. (1992) *Stretching the Subject: The Subject Organization of High Schools and the Transformation of Work Education.* Berkeley, CA: National Centre for Research Education.

Lohnes, S. (2003) *Weblogs in Education: Bringing the World to the Liberal Arts Classroom.* The Newsletter of the National Institute for Technology and Liberal Education 2(1). Accessed 31 May 2006 from <http://newsletter.nitle.org/v2_n1_winter2003/features_weblogs.php>.

Lorenzo, G. and Ittelson, J. (2005) 'An overview of Institutional e-portfolios', in D. Oblinger (ed.) *Educause Learning Initiative.* Available online at: <http://www.educause.edu/ir/library/pdf/ELI3002.pdf> (accessed 28 April 2006).

MacDonald, J. (2004) 'Developing competent e-learners: the role of assessment', *Assessment and Evaluation in Higher Education* 29(2): 215–226.

Maher, P. (2001) 'The Open University's portfolio approach to personal and career development', in C. Juwah, L.A.J. Stefani, J. Westwood, C. Gray and J. Drysdale (eds) *Personal Development Planning in Practice: A Series of Case Studies*. Aberdeen: CLASS.

Mason, R. (2002) 'E-learning: what have we learnt? Improving student learning using learning technologies', *Proceedings, 9th Improving Student Learning Symposium, 2001*, 27–34.

Mason, R.D., Pegler, C.A. and Weller, M.J. (2004) 'E-portfolios: an assessment tool for online courses', *British Journal of Educational Technology* 35(6): 717–727.

McConnell, D. (2000) *Implementing Computer Supported Co-operative Learning* (2nd edn). London: Kogan Page.

MERLOT – Multimedia Educational Resource for Learning and Online Teaching. Available online at: <http://www.merlot.org>.

Miller, A., Imnie, B. and Cox, K. (1998) *Student Assessment in Higher Education*. London: Kogan Page.

Moon, J. (2005) 'Learning through reflection', Higher Education Academy Guide for Busy Academics No. 4. Available online at: <http://www.heacademy.ac.uk/resources.asp?process=full_record&section=generic&id=69> (accessed 21 December 2005).

Morgaine, W. and Angell, N. (2006) *Integrating Portfolios with OSP at Portland State*. Available online at: <http://www.cfkeep.org.html/snapshot.php?id=763916170936> (accessed 30 May 2006).

Myers, J. (1991) 'Co-operative learning in heterogeneous classes', *Co-operative Learning* 11(4): 36–48.

Nuventive (2006) 'Electronic portfolio solutions: performance and requirements analysis checklist.' Available online at: <http://www.nuventive.com/ElectronicPortfolioAnalysisTool.pdf>.

Oblinger, D. and Hawkins, B. (2006) 'The myth about online course development', *Educause Review* 41(1): 14–15.

O'Hear, S. (2005a) *E-learning, Seconds out, round two*. Available online at: <http://education.guardian.co.uk/elearning/story/0,10577,1642281,00.html>.

O'Hear, S. (2005b) 'Podcasts offer the audience pupils crave'. Available online at: <http://education.guardian.co.uk/elearning/story/0,1583830,00.htm> (accessed 28 April 2006).

Oliver, M. (1996) *Understanding disability: from theory to practice*. London/Basingstoke: Palgrave Press.

OSPI, Open Source Portfolio Initiative. Available online at: <http://www.osportfolio.org/> (accessed 20 May 2006).

O'Suilleabhain, G. (2004) 'The convergence of e-learning and higher education', *WebCT (2004) Conference Amsterdam*. Available online at: <http://webct. com/europe2004> (accessed 28 April 2006).

Peat, M. and Franklin, S. (2002) 'Supporting student learning: the use of computer-based formative assessment modules', *British Journal of Educational Technology* 33(5): 517–526.

Prensky M. (2001) 'Digital natives, digital immigrants', *On the Horizon* 9(5) October. Available online at: <http://www.marcprensky.com/writing/Prensky%20-%20Digital%20Natives,%20Digital%20Immigrants%20-%20Part1.pdf>.

QAA (1999) Code of practice for the assurance of academic quality and standards in higher education. Section 3: Students with disabilities. October. Available online at: <http://www.qaa.ac.uk/academicinfrastructure/progressfiles/guidelines.pdf>.

QAA (2001) Available online at: <http://www.qaa.ac.uk/academic infrastructure /progressFiles/guidelines/progfile2001.pdf> (accessed 10 November 2005).

Qualifications and Curriculum Authority (2004) 'A proposed blueprint for delivering e-assessment'. Available online at: <http://www.qca.org.uk/downloads/6995_blueprint_for_e-assessment.rtf>.

Rainger, P. (2003) A dyslexic perspective on e-content accessibility. Available online at <http://old.techdis.ac.uk/seven/papers/dyslexia. html> (accessed 04 January 2007).

Ramsden, P. (2003) *Learning to Teach in Higher Education* (2ⁿᵈ edn). London and New York: Routledge & Falmer.

Regosin, E. (n.d.) Academic planning at SLU: cultivating intentionality. Available online at: <http.//www.stlawu.edu/acadaffairs/academic%20planning%20at%20slu.pdf> (Accessed 22 December 2005).

Rennie, F. and Mason, R. (2004) *The Connecticon: Learning for the Connected Generation.* Charlotte, NC: Information Age Publishing.

Rheingold, H. (2002) *Smart Mobs: The next social revolution.* New York: Perseus Publishing.

Sabre, J.M. (2002) 'A conversation with Jeannette Mercer Sabre'. Available online at: <http://portfolio.psu.edu/faculty/course/feature4.html> (accessed 22 December 2005).

Sakai: Collaboration and Learning Environment for Education. Available online at: <http://www.sakaiproject.org>.

Scott Morton, M.S. (1991) 'Introduction', in M.S. Scott Morton (ed.) *The Corporation of the 1990s USA.* Oxford University Press.

Seldin, P. (1997) *The Teaching Portfolio: A Practical Guide to Improved Performance and Promotion/Tenure Decisions* (2ⁿᵈ edn). Bolton, MA: Anker Publishing Inc.

Seymour, W. and Lupton, D. (2004) 'Holding the line online: exploring wired relationships for people with disabilities', *Disability and Society* 19(4): 291–305.

Shakespeare, T. (2005) Different Differences, Partners in Practice Project. Available online at: <http://www.bris.ac.uk/pip/>.

Siemens, G. (2004) 'E-portfolios' – accessed from *elearnspace.* Available online at: <http://www.elearnspace.org/Articles/eportfolios.htm> (accessed 22 May 2006).

Singleton, C (1999) *The Report of the National Working Party on Dyslexia in Higher Education.* Hull: University of Hull (ISBN 1 898862 99 0).

Skills for Access: *The Comprehensive Guide to Creating Accessible Multimedia for e-Learning.* Available online at: <http://www.skillsforaccess.org.uk> (accessed 01 February 2006).

Slavin, R. (1994) 'Student teams and achievement divisions', in S. Sharon (ed.) *Handbook of Cooperative Learning Methods.* Westport, CT: Greenwood Press, 3–19.

Snadden, D., Thomas, M. and Challis, M.C. (1999) *AMEE Education Guide No 11: Portfolio-based Learning and Assessment.* Dundee: Association for Medical Education in Europe.

SPIDER: Pharmacy Website, University of Strathclyde, Glasgow, Scotland. Available online at: <http://www.spider.pharmacy.strath.ac.uk>.

St Olaf College Centre for Integrative Studies: *Web portfolios, Enhancing the Coherence of Students' Careers.* Available online at: <http://www.stolaf.edu /depts/cis/web_portfolios.htm>.

Stacey, E. (1998) 'Learning collaboratively in a CMC environment', in G. Davies (ed.) *Teleteaching 98: Distance Learning, Training and Education, Proceedings of the XV IFIP World Computer Congress,* 951–960, Vienna and Budapest.

Stanford Learning Laboratory E-Folio. Available online at: <http://sll.stanford. edu/consulting/tools/efolio> (accessed 24 May 2006).

Stanford University Learning Laboratory. Available online at: <http://see-stan-dord.edu/consulting/tools/efolio> (accessed 01 December 2005).

Stefani, L.A.J. (1998) 'Assessment in partnership with learners', *Assessment and Evaluation in Higher Education,* 23(4): 339–350.

Stefani, L.A.J. (2004) 'Assessment of student learning: promoting a scholarly approach', *Learning and Teaching in Higher Education* 1(1): 51–66.

Stefani, L.A.J. (2005) 'Towards a shared understanding of scholarship in the classroom', in P. Ashwin (ed.) *Changing Higher Education: The Development of Learning and Teaching.* London: Routledge, 113–124.

Stefani, L.A.J. and Diener, S. (2005) 'The e-Teaching portfolio as a tool to promote professional development', Proceedings of Educause 2005. ISBN 0 86869-108-9.

Stefani, L.A.J. and Elton, L. (2002) 'Continuing professional development of academic teachers through self-initiated learning', *Assessment and Evaluation in Higher Education* 27(2): 117–129.

Stefani, L.A.J. and Nicol, D. (1997) 'From teacher to facilitator of collaborative learning', in S. Armstrong, G. Thompson and S. Brown (eds) *Facing up to Radical Changes in Universities and Colleges.* London: Kogan Page, 131–140.

Steyaert, J. (2005) 'Web-based higher education, the inclusion/exclusion paradox', *Journal of Technology in Human Services* 23(1): 67–78.

Taite, T. (2000) 'General strategies for revising and editing on computers', *Literacy Education Online.* Available online at: <http://leo.stcloudstate.edu /acadwrite/computerediting.html> (accessed 20 February 2006).

Tartwijk, J. van and Driessen, E. (2004) European Portfolio Initiatives Co-ordination Committee. Available online at: <http://www.epiccproject.info> (accessed 22 May 2006).

Teachability Project (2000) University of Strathclyde. Available online at: <http://www.teachability.strath.ac.uk> (accessed 29 May 2006).

TechDis (2003) 'A Dyslexic Perspective on e-Content Accessibility' (Rainger, P.F.) Available online at: <http:/www.techdis.ac.uk/sevenpapers/> (accessed 10 February 2006).

TechDis (2004) 'Accessibility do's and don'ts for beginners'. Available online at: <http://www.techdis.ac.uk/index.php?p=1_20040511081154_20042411011 107> (accessed 20 February 2006).

TechDis. Available online at: <http://www.techdis.ac.uk> (accessed 29 May 2006).

Tosh, D. and Werdmuller, B. (2005) 'Creation of a learning landscape: homogenizing weblogging, social networking and e-portfolios'. Paper presented at ePortfolio 2005, Cambridge, October 26–8, 143–149.

Trehan, K. and Reynolds, M. (2002) 'Online collaborative assessment: power relations and "critical learning"', in C. Steeples and C. Jones (eds) *Networked Learning Perspectives and Issues,* London: Springer Verlag, 280.

Treuer, P. and Jensen, J.D. (2003) 'Electronic portfolios need standards to thrive', EDUCAUSE Quarterly 2: 34–42.

Underwood, J.D.M. and Dillon, G. (2004) 'Maturity modelling: a framework for capturing the effects of technology', *Pedagogy and Education* 13(2): 213–225

University of British Columbia (UBC) (2005) Department of Pharmaceutical Sciences. Available online at: <http://weblogs.elearning.ubc.ca/projectportfolio/archives/projects/pharmaceutical_sciences/> (accessed 25 January 2006).

User Land Software. Available online at: <http://www.userland.com>.

Veugelers, M., Aalderink, W., Kemps, A., Meeder, S., Tartwijk, J. van and Veltman, F. (2004) 'e-Portfolios in the Netherlands and the UK'. Briefing Paper for the ALT-SURF seminar: ePortfolios and Digital Repositories, Edinburgh. Available online at: <http://www.surf.nl/en/download/ALT-SURF_seminar_April_2004. pdf>.

Vygotsky, L. (1978) *Mind in Society.* Cambridge, MA: Harvard University Press.

W3C Web Accessibility Initiative (last update September 2005). Available online at: <http://www.w3.org/WAI/> (accessed 27 February 2006).

Wade, A., Abrami, P. and Sclater, J. (2005) 'An electronic portfolio to support learning', *Canadian Journal of Learning and Technology* 31(3). Available online at: <http://www.cjlt.ca/content/vol31.3/wade.html>.

Wiles, K. (2002) Accessibility and computer-based asssessment: a whole new set of issues? In L. Phipps, A. Sutherland, and J. Seale (eds), *Access all areas: disability, technology and learning.* JISC, TechDis Service and ALT.

Wilkinson, L. (n.d.) How to build scenarios. Available online at <http://www.wired.com/wired/scenarios/build.html>.

World Wide Web Consortium. Available online at: <http://www.w3.org/> (accessed 27 February 2006).

Yancey, K.B. (2001) 'Digitized student portfolios', in B. Cambridge (ed.) *Electronic Portfolios: Emerging Practices in Student, Faculty and Institutional Learning.* Washington, DC: American Association of Higher Education, 83–87.

Yorke, M. and Knight, P. (2004) *Learning, Curriculum and Employability in Higher Education.* London: Routledge Falmer.

Index